New York City's Best Dive Bars:
Drinking & Diving in the Five Boroughs

Wendy Mitchell

A Gamble Guide

Ig Publishing, New York

New York City's Best Dive Bars:
Drinking & Diving in the Five Boroughs

Published in New York
by Gamble Guides

Gamble Guides is an imprint of
Ig Publishing
www.igpub.com

ISBN 0-9703125-3-9

10 9 8 7 6 5 4 3 2

Photography by Swan

Cover Design by Chris Kornmann for spit and image

Cover photograph of Johnny's Bar, 90 Greenwich Avenue, New York City, printed with permission

*For all my favorite drinking buddies,
you know who you are*

Red Rock West Saloon

Why Dive Bars?

Anyone who has ever spent a few nights in a claustrophobic Manhattan studio apartment knows why New Yorkers hold their bars so dear in their hearts and livers. New Yorkers don't (and can't) gather *in* their apartments, they gather *out* of them. For those of us with limited space, your local bar can effectively function as your living room (or your post office: I know of some regulars who have gotten their mail delivered at their favorite watering hole). And, for those of us on a limited salary and an unlimited thirst for alcohol and trouble, there is no better place to find it than in a New York City dive bar! These aging, filthy relics are a reminder of a classic New York, a place before Times Square was taken over by Disney, a place before a pack of cigarettes cost seven dollars, a place where grit and dirt were a sign of character. You can find a dance club in Tokyo or a lounge in London, but a seedy dive feels like the missing link to old New York, to a time when men were men and girls were dames. Sometimes, yes, I want to throw on some strappy heels and go dancing at Plant or sip lychee martinis at Kin Khao. But most of the time, I'm content on a tattered bar stool with a can of cheap beer and some interesting, if slightly slurred, conversation.

Long before the idea for this book was spawned, I was a dive barfly. During my first summer in New York City, back in the mid-nineties, my fake ID bought me many shots of fun at the now-defunct Phebe's on the Bowery. When I moved here for good in 1996, I immediately eschewed nights at Spy or Pravda for five dollar pitchers at the now sadly closed Boo Radley's. After much exploring and imbibing, I discovered my two all-time favorite dives, Siberia (near work), and Johnny's (near home). Many of my friends were at first repulsed by these fine barely standing establishments, but they soon came around to my way of thinking and my style of drinking.

Sadly, the gentrification that has hit New York City over the past decade has turned many classic dives into lounges where investment bankers sip cosmos while hitting on wannabe models. These places are fine if you're in the mood and have the cash, but sometimes you just need a shot of adventure with a beer chaser. Sometimes you need a bar older than yourself (and older than your father and grandfather), a place where you're scared to get *tooo* friendly with the regulars, and even more scared to sit on the toilet seat. Sometimes you need to drink a cheap draft from an unwashed glass, and in the process rediscover a little piece of real New

Bathroom of Sweetwater Tavern

York, untouched by time or cleaning solution. So pull up a broken stool, order a Bud on tap, and avoid making eye contact with the guy with one tooth smiling at you from the other end of the bar. Welcome to New York City's Best Dive Bars!

Wendy Mitchell
October, 2002

Wendy's 10 Rules On What Constitutes A Dive Bar

1) There needs to be an old man at the bar who looks like he's in there every night, or at least the bar should look like an old man might wander in at any moment. A grimy place that's filled with 22-year-old hipsters doesn't count.

2) Real dive bars typically don't serve food beyond pretzels and such. Maybe some chicken wings, but no "real" food (there are a few notable exceptions—Ear Inn, Emerald Inn, so on).

3) If barkeeps are charging $7 for a bottle of beer, or you notice that most drinks are being served in martini glasses, you're not in a dive.

4) If you'd be scared to take your parents there, it's a dive.

5) If your parents would be worried sick if they knew you hung out there, it's a dive.

6) It's all about the crowd! A place can have candles with fresh flowers at the bar, but if there's a toothless old geezer talking about some guy he offed in the '50s, it's a dive.

7) In a real dive, you don't feel weird ordering a drink 10 minutes after you ordered the previous one. Nobody's gonna roll their eyes at you if you have a high tolerance and a quick intake.

8) If the bathroom's clean, it's not a dive.

9) In most cases, a dive can't be "new." It needs a few years under its belt to accumulate grime, puke, and a regular crowd.

10) If you can't get a bottle of Bud, it's not a dive.

About the "Dive Factor"

I ranked the bars in this book on a scale of general "diviness"—1 to 10. 1 is relatively harmless, 5 would be a great place to go with open-minded friends, and 10 equals a place where you may want to be packing heat.

But What About . . . ?

What's included and what's not:

There are a few great bars that aren't exactly swank but still didn't make my cut. For starters, CBGB and the Continental are great music bars, not just dive bars. Still, they are worth a visit.

Standard Irish pubs tend to be a little too clean and same-y to be divey.

There are places that can be a teensy bit rough around the edges, which I just consider to be neighborhood places—Spring Lounge, Ace Bar, etc.

Lastly, there are some extremely divey joints (I remember one place in Greenpoint with an octogenarian "singer" at a Casio keyboard, taking requests from sleazy and saggy Polish women clad in stretch pants) that I just wouldn't consider the city's *best* dives.

If you have suggestions for future editions, we'd love to hear from you: divebars@hotmail.com.

Tips For Successful Diving

1) Tip well. Your drinks are cheap, and as my wise friend Michelle taught me: nobody ever got rich by stiffing a bartender or a cabdriver. Plus good tips bode well for buybacks.

2) Stick to something with one mixer—cranberry juice, tonic, whatever.

3) If the draft beer tastes a little gross, suck it up. If it tastes a lot gross, get a replacement.

4) Always sit at the bar—it's more interesting.

5) No matter how many pals you're with, talk to at least one stranger.

6) Shell out a few bucks to put plenty of songs on the jukebox; it's always good to hear your faves when you're a bit tipsy. Don't try to sing along—if this were karaoke, you'd have a microphone.

7) Don't be afraid to stay out after your friends go home; you'll have some fun stories to make them jealous the following day.

8) Don't be persuaded into bar dancing if you're not the type—you'll just end up looking silly.

9) Inter-bar dating is like inter-office dating. If you hook up with a bartender or a regular, and things go sour, you may have to find a new hangout.

10) Stay out until 4 a.m. on a weeknight once in a while. The hangover will be manageable and you'll feel like a rebel while sitting at your desk the next day.

New York's 10 Best Dive Bars
(in alphabetical order)

Blue & Gold
The quintessential East Village dive, with dirt *and* dirt-cheap drinks

Freddy's
A Brooklyn classic worth the trek from Manhattan

Grassroots Tavern
A subterranean hideout on St. Mark's Place

Jimmy's Corner
An old, cheap watering hole near Times Square

Johnny's
A character-filled hole-in-the-wall in the West Village

Mare Chiaro
An old Italian oasis where Tony Soprano would feel right at home

Mars Bar
A bar that has earned its reputation as NY's diviest dive

Red Rock West
A true biker bar way over on 10th Avenue

Rudy's
The perfect American combo of pitchers and hot dogs in Hell's Kitchen

Siberia
The former subway station bar now has roomier digs but the same cool crowd

NEW YORK CITY'S BEST DIVE BARS

(IN ALPHABETICAL ORDER)

Alibi

718-783-8519
242 DeKalb Avenue, at Vanderbilt Avenue, Clinton Hill, Brooklyn
Subway Directions: C or G to Clinton-Washington Avenues

Alibi is a bit out of the way, and seems to like it that way. However, it is well worth the Magellan-like voyage to this unmarked bar in the Clinton Hill/Fort Greene section of Brooklyn. The first thing I always notice when I walk in is how old I feel. Not that I am *that* old, mind you, but the crowd is decidedly collegiate—mostly from the nearby Pratt College of Art. The second thing I notice is the cute artsy boys (and then I have to remind myself to keep my hands off anyone barely of legal drinking age). The third thing I notice is that the place is so thick with smoke that you can hardly see in front of your face. But hey, two out of three ain't bad. Physically, the space doesn't teem with character—the front room is slightly subterranean, albeit with a nice old wooden bar and a prime front table by the bay window. There's also a pool table that draws a steady crowd of non-Pratt locals. The jukebox, while overpriced, has an outstanding mix of indie rock, Brit Invasion classics, and even some rather cutting-edge dance tunes.

The types I have encountered here include one of those aforementioned art students, who was eager for my whole posse to sign his drawing tablet (not sure why), and a chap who took over the back room one Saturday night and proceeded to play some terribly off-kilter classical pieces on the terribly out of tune piano, despite the fact that a punk song was already blaring form the jukebox. When the back room en masse asked him to stop, he told us to "get the hell out if we didn't want to hear some *good* music."

Perks: pool table, varied jukebox, piano in the back room, cute boys and girls everywher, a back "garden" (of the cement variety) where you can chill in the summer and watch the kiddies pass around funny smelling cigarettes

Dive factor: 6

American Trash

212-988-9008
1471 First Avenue, between 76th and 77th Street
Subway Directions: 6 to 77th Street

American Trash certainly lives up to its name—unfortunately it's indicative of the clientele rather than the décor. Bras up on the moosehead and guys in cowboy boots demonstrate a valiant attempt to give the place that country dive flavor, but the too-bright lighting and a lack of sufficient smoke in the air make this bar feel more like Hogs & Heifers Lite than the down home roadhouse it aspires to be. But the mixed clientele is plenty divey. Two Jersey Shore-type couples groping each other at the next table, and a guy in sweatshorts (to quote George Costanza, sweatpants just tell the world you've given up) had my posse fleeing this place fairly quickly in search of denim and downtown.

Not one of the city's best dives, but if you're stuck on the Upper East Side, it'll do. The $8 deal on six Rolling Rock ponies makes it more bearable, as do the nightly $2 specials. The jukebox is a decent mix of hard rock (Metallica, Ozzy), jukebox classics (Bob Marley, the Beatles) and a few surprises (My Life with the Thrill Kill Kult). Be warned that AC/DC inspires the gold-chained set to air guitar.

This themey dive on the Upper East Side is a great find for women with fake tans and the men who love them.

Perks: video games, pool, TVs

Dive factor: 5

Smokiest Dives

Alibi
Sophie's
Lucy's
Milano
Mona's
Subway Inn

Baby Doll Lounge

Baby Doll Lounge

212-226-4870
34 White Street, at Church Street
Subway Directions: A/C/E to Canal Street, 1/2 to Franklin Street

A friend described his first visit to the Baby Doll, which was in fact his first visit to any strip club, as a virtual "mugging." Through a communication mix-up in those pre-cell phone days of yesteryear, he arrived three hours early for a bachelor party, visions of velvet ropes and buxom blondes dancing in his head. Instead, he walked into this one-room girlie bar and saw some, to be delicate, "less-than-perfect" ladies gyrating for two members of the elderly set who sat slumped and glass-eyed over their beers. While he waited for his friends, he tried to keep his head down so the dancing queens wouldn't hit him up for cash. It didn't work. Every time he glanced up (which was easy to do, considering the mirror behind the bar), a dancer would expect $5 to be stuffed into her bikini. To make matters worse, the one dancer he found mildly attractive had a huge, ragged scar running from her throat to her bellybutton. Another pal reports that one of his friends was last seen alive at the Baby Doll—when he was found dead in his apartment, all that was on his person was heroin and a receipt from Baby Doll.

Scores it ain't, but Baby Doll still has plenty of character, and the beers won't empty your wallet like the strippers. Plus there's pinball for the ladies. Like Billy's Topless, Guiliana-era reforms mean that the Baby Dolls can't go topless, but at least the Baby Doll survives (unlike Billy's in Chelsea, which became "Stopless" and then had to completely shut its doors). In another interesting juxtaposition of old New York meets new New York, the overly swank Tribeca Grand hotel, with its sprawling lounge, is located a stone's throw away.

Rumor has it that Soft Cell's "Baby Doll" was based on this joint.

Perks: pinball, T&A

Dive factor: 8

The Bar

212-254-5766
68 Second Avenue, at 4th Street
Subway Directions: 6 to Astor Place

Despite the gothic letters painted on the sign outside, The Bar is a nod to a Western roadhouse, or a big gay log cabin nestled in the East Village. A distinctly no-frills establishment, The Bar is more low-key than its sister (or perhaps brother would be more accurate) bar, The Boiler Room, around the corner. The Bar varies from night to night, with a mixed crowd—old-timers, young studs, and on a night when I visited, a pair of octogenarian women. My friend Brian once had somebody accidentally light his hair on fire in here, and—only in New York—struck up a friendly chat with the inflaming party.

The décor is a mixed bag—*Charlie's Angels*-inspired globe lights, lots and lots of wood, neon Camel signs, jazz posters, and some original art that was either depicting an alien or Michael Stipe (no offense to my man Stipe, it's just hard to tell what the artist was going for). Even though our mixed drinks were tasty, The Bar is definitely located more in the Budweiser zone.

Judging from the 11 kamikaze shots the bartender made for our gang in rapid-fire succession, The Bar is a great place to bring a large group, or perhaps your next gay corporate event. For the ladies or shy men, note that only one bathroom has a lock. But the crowd is pretty controlled and polite. (One outward sign of that politeness: the suggestion box on the bar.) And on Monday nights, a bit of Eurotrash culture hits The Bar, as a "Moulin Rouge" theme night offers Francophile pop.

Perks: pool, jukebox

Dive factor: 7

Barrows Pub

463 Hudson Street, at Barrow Street
212-741-9349
Subway Directions: A/C/E to 14th Street, 1/2 to Christopher Street

My friend Bill and his cousin Kitty nicknamed this place the "Twin Peaks" Bar. The place is a bit Lynchian—among the regulars are One-Armed Joe From the Alamo, and Tonto, a musician who used to play with Tito Puente. It's also one of the friendliest and most unpretentious bars in NYC. Definitely not a tourist spot, the clientele consists of West Village regulars looking for a good no-frills time. However, even outsiders like myself are made to feel welcome by the patrons and the chatty, girl-next-door bartender.

The jukebox is surprisingly good, featuring such goodies as the cheesy dance song "C'Mon and Ride the Train," which Bill and I once played to the chagrin of the sane patrons. If you're hungry, you can get some pizza (probably not hand-tossed in the back). Happy hour (4-7 weekdays) is a bargain, and prices are affordable at other hours of the day and night. Just don't try to order a cosmo or run a tab—the sign behind the bar says "no tabs/no credit/money on the wood." If you're in a betting mood, you can try your luck at the Quick Draw machine. But a word of warning—the dangerous combination of cheap drinks, an ATM machine, and legalized gambling could force you to sign up for both Alcoholics *and* Gamblers Anonymous.

Perks: jukebox, pool, pizza, Quick Draw, ATM machine, dog-friendly (the bartenders are free and easy with the Milkbones)

Dive factor: 7

Bar 81 (Verk)

212-598-4394
81 East Seventh Street, at First Avenue
Subway Directions: F/V to Second Avenue, 6 to Astor Place

The sign out front might say Bar 81, but most of us call this bare bones establishment "the Verk," short for the lettering in the windows, Verkhovyna Tavern, which tells much about this place's old-school Ukrainian heritage. The Verk is conveniently located amidst a strip of hotspots that also includes Tile Bar, Big Bar, and Blue and Gold, so it makes for an ideal starting or ending place for your night on the town. The bartenders are no-nonsense but affable, and the bottled beer is a steal compared to the prices at nearby bars.

The place doesn't have many frills, other than a fairly predictable, but likable, jukebox and a pool table. But its small space makes it intimate—there are just a few stools at the bar and a few booths alongside, so if you're standing, you'll be mingling whether you like it or not. The crowd is quite friendly—whether it's the young NYU types, the crusty old man carrying his baguette around with him, or the visiting British couple who just wanted some suggestions on where to eat Indian food and score some pot. With that old Ukrainian hospitality rubbing off on us, my friends and I tried to point them in the right direction for both their requests.

The place is great for wasting away a few hours, although after a few rounds, you'll be ready to hop to new surroundings. But drink cheap while you can. It's amazing how quickly one of those Formica tables can be completely covered with beer bottles if you've got the right drinking partners with you. Note that they don't take too kindly to dancing—during one of the recent Yankees World Series games, a pal of mine and his friends kept infuriating the bartender with their boogieing until he told them it was illegal for more than one person to be dancing at a time. They promptly annoyed him even more when they started tag-team dancing.

Perks: jukebox, pool

Dive factor: 7

Bellevue

212-760-0660
538 Ninth Avenue, at 40th Street
Subway Directions: A/C/E to 42nd Street/Port Authority

My two favorite things about Bellevue are the way-cool bartenders (very personable, and willing to flash their bras if you're into that kind of thing) and the fact that you can buy a can, or a dozen cans, of Pabst.

The place was an old Hell's Kitchen haunt that lived through many lives and was refurbished and renamed in 1997 by Siberia's Tracy Westmoreland. The result is half Hell's Kitchen seediness, half kitschiness. Among the homages to kitsch kool that litter the bar are a bust of Elvis, lava lamps, weightlifting trophies, Halloween masks enshrined in cases, and framed, doctored ads from Bellevue Hospital.

The Bellevue crowd is a combination of suits from neighboring businesses, old metalheads drinking the day away, goth kids, and the occasional Port Authority straggler (I once—and thankfully only once—saw a patron clipping his toenails at the bar). The TV sometimes features '70's porn flicks, and the jukebox is always ready to pump out some beefy classic rock—where else can you find a Scorpions CD? If that's not enough for you, then the rambunctious barkeeps are always ready to pour you a mean shot.

A few years ago, when I worked at a dot-com related business a few blocks away, we'd come to Bellevue at least once a week to drown our sorrows about the hassles of our jobs. These days, after the dot-com bust and my corresponding dot-canning, I still return on a regular basis, as the kitsch, leather, bra straps and, of course, Pabst Blue Ribbon, somehow make for a surprisingly cheerful mixture. And if you discover Bellevue isn't your scene, its evil twin sister Siberia is just around the corner.

Perks: jukebox, Ms. Pac-Man, the fact that one of my friends thought that Bellevue was the perfect place to shoot up hormones in the bathroom (she was selling her eggs at the time)

Dive Factor: 7

Bellevue

Between the Bridges

718-237-1977
63 York Street, at Adams Street, DUMBO, Brooklyn
Subway Directions: F to York Street

I learned about Between the Bridges from a rather unique woman who lived in upstate New York but was down in DUMBO couch-surfing while she sold vintage evening wear that used to belong to a dead acquaintance. She was biding her time (and money) in New York City, and was thrilled to discover the free afternoon buffet at Between the Bridges.

As you would expect from its name, BTB is located between the Brooklyn and Manhattan Bridges, and while it's not waterfront property, you get a cool view as you're walking to the bar from the F train. (And if you could afford waterfront, you'd be sipping wine at the River Café, wouldn't you?) Despite DUMBO's increasing gentrification, the place remains laid-back, with a mix of blue-collar types and some of the more relaxed artist folk who live in the area. It opens at 10 a.m. for those souls who don't hold down day jobs. Be sure to grab a seat on the patio outside—it's not lush, but it's still outdoors.

Perks: outdoor patio, free buffet, TVs, occasional live music

Dive factor: 4

On The Waterfront
(or at least Near the Water-front)

Sand Bar
Johnny's Reef
Jeremy's
Montero
Sneakers
Between the Bridges
Ruby's

Billymark's West

212-620-0118
332 Ninth Avenue, at 29th Street
Subway Directions: C/E to 23rd Street, A/C/E to 34th Street

Billymark's clientele seemingly strolls in from the local projects across the street. Folks seem friendly enough, but the crowd is definitely a bit rough around the edges—best not to stir up too much trouble here (unless someone's got your back). However, the slightly scary aura lends an edginess to the place, which makes it feel like an honest-to-goodness dive, not a marketing executive's idea of a dive.

The mixed drinks are small but fairly potent, and we also spied not one but two flavors of that ghetto libation Alizé behind the bar. Our Absolut Mandarin and tonics were only $3.50 but the glasses appeared to need a good rinse and the tonic was flat. Oh well, did I mention they were only $3.50?

The real draw at Billymark's is a surprisingly kick-ass jukebox, which boasts tons of classic rock and British invasion staples (wouldn't have pegged the patrons to belong to the *Rubber Soul* set), plus some inspired picks from other genres (Tower of Power, Billie Holiday, Joe Jackson, Mary J. Blige, Peaches & Herb (!), Elvis Costello, etc.). I suggest you bring your posse, settle in at the bar, steer clear of the dart games, and just pump the jukebox full of tunes. Heed the sign posted behind the bar: "Clothing optional/ Drinking mandatory."

Perks: darts, jukebox, would be an ideal place to shoot up some smack if only you didn't have to be buzzed into the ladies room!

Dive factor: 9

Best Reasons to Leave Manhattan

Johnny's Famous Reef (Bronx)
Bohemian Hall & Beer Garden (Queens)
Sidestreet Saloon (Staten Island)
Freddy's (Brooklyn)

Blarney Cove

212-473-9284
510 E. 14th Street, between Avenues A and B
Subway Directions: L to First Avenue

In a city of homogenized bars, the Blarney Cove stands apart as a true one-of-a-kind (please don't get it confused with similarly named chains like Blarney Stone and the Blarney Rock). The Cove is a bar from another time and another New York (it opened almost 40 years ago), and it's easy to lose track of time here, as well as sobriety and eventually, consciousness. The gentlemen of a certain age behind the bar know how to treat you right. They're up for a chat if you are, or they'll leave you alone if you're occupied with other things. In the wee hours, the dingy realm actually has a sort of club vibe to it—the long, skinny shape of the place means that anybody passing through basically bumps into everybody already there, so there's plenty of mingling opportunities. It's up to you whether you want to get to know these folks—a few neighborhood vipers, tired club-hoppers, blue collar workers, and whoever the hell else has washed on the shore of the Cove. The dynamic crowd means it's never the same place twice—so you may have to log in a few visits before you have a raucous evening here.

As an added bonus for the strong-stomached, the barkeeps occasionally have some kind of foot-long sub sitting out for you to graze on for free. My friend Robert ate it heartily, and survived quite nicely. If you're faint of heart, stay to the front of the bar, because the seedier types are usually lurking in the back area by the bathrooms. And please, tip your hat to my pal Matt, who hangs out here so much that his nickname has become "Captain Cove."

Perks: jukebox, occasional free sandwich, TVs, and as one good friend put it, the Cove is a perfect place to "wash up" on the tail end of a long drinking binge

Dive factor: 8

Blue and Gold Tavern

212-473-8918
79 East 7th Street, between First and Second Avenue
Subway Directions: F/V to Second Avenue, 6 to Astor Place

B&G probably isn't my first choice to spend an entire evening in if it's crowded with youngsters, but it's still a great place to wile away a few hours. The central East Village location makes it a prime stop on a crawl that could begin or end at the nearby Verk, or Tile Bar. The youngish crowd, some definitely still in college, made me at first acutely aware of my almost thirty years. But after a few of the minimally priced drinks, I felt like I was 21 again.

Nearly everybody I know has a fondness for this place—one friend met a boyfriend in here, one met her favorite "salesman" here, and one boldly picked up someone else's date and took her home. No matter what the goings on, the Ukranian women behind the bar remain stone-faced and focused on one thing—mixing those *$3* cocktails!

The bathrooms are rather small, especially the ladies', but that didn't stop a certain friend of mine from getting it on with not one but two gents simultaneously. Recent décor improvements include a custom Lite Brite sign in the window, and the removal of layers of grime on the folksy murals adorning the walls (think of it as the same way they removed all that grime from the Sistine Chapel, only this grime was probably beer residue, smoke, puke, and other things decidedly un-Christian).

The Blue and Gold is a great place for a little bit of decadence on a weekday night, for starting off your Saturday night, or even for starting early on a Sunday. No matter what you are looking for—trouble, love, candy, a hangover you won't soon forget or remember—you'll be able to find it, cheaply, at the B&G.

Perks: pool, excellent locale, good jukebox (if you are lucky, you may be treated to an impromptu Bon Jovi group sing-along)

Dive factor: 8

Bohemian Hall and Beer Garden

718-274-4925
29-12 Twenty-Fourth Avenue, between 29th and 31st Street, Astoria, Queens
Subway Directions: N/W to Astoria Boulevard

Only a few New Yorkers have backyards, so outdoor drinking in the city usually involves small cement patios or brown bags in Central Park. Thank heaven the Beer Garden shares its patch of land with us poor gardenless souls. This gigantic indoor and outdoor bar complex, which holds 1000 people, is unique not only for its size and construction (its cornerstone was laid in 1910), but because it is run by the Bohemian Citizens Benevolent Society, a society that easily predates 1910. In fact, it looks as if some of the original Bohemian Citizens are still drinking at the indoor bar.

Czech and Slovak immigrants will feel especially welcome, as most workers speak Czech (and fortunately, English). The regulars consist of middle-aged and elderly immigrants, along with a more-than-generous sampling of the rest of the eclectic neighborhood folk. On a Sunday afternoon visit, I spotted a bickering hipster couple, a family filming their newborn baby, a group of young Greek guys downing pitchers, and a huge extended family celebrating a christening.

The Hall often hosts holiday parties and ethnic festivals, and the band shell and dance area of the garden welcomes local jazz groups, Czech rock bands, and even touring acts like the Samples. The main indoor bar is a dark, wooden room with a jukebox and mementos of the Czech Republic. A newly added second indoor bar has DJs on Saturdays after 10 who play an innovative mix of techno and Czech "classics." Outside, the no-frills picnic tables, settled on gravel, make a great place for a group gathering. Of course, when the crowds hit you may have to wait for your beer or the old-world food (goulash, kielbasa and various schnitzels are served on weekends). After a few pitchers, you will forget that the N train and the Triboro bridge are just steps away from this oasis. Open Monday through Friday, 5 p.m. 'til 3 a.m., and Saturday and Sunday from noon 'til 3 a.m.

Perks: live music, food on weekends, outdoor seating

Dive factor: 2

Boiler Room

212-254-7536
86 E. 4th Street, between 1st and 2nd Avenue
Subway Directions: F/V to Second Avenue, 6 to Astor Place

I like *Golden Girls* reruns as much as any gay man I know, but that doesn't necessarily mean I want to hang out in Dorothy and Blanche's living room. I tell you this because this East Village gay bar has a, shall we say, "strange" amalgam of decorating styles—and one corner looks suspiciously like grandma's Florida retirement village hand-me-downs. The rest of the place is equally representative of the motto "let us mix, but not match:" hideous Greco-Roman columns painted on one wall, pleather couches in clusters, and a cheesy fake castle around the DJ booth. All of this unstyle is okay, though, because on weekends the place will be so packed you won't be able to even see the décor.

My experts assure me that the Boiler Room used to be a must-visit stop on the downtown gay bar circuit, but today it has lost its luster. Tourists and the less-hip are the norm now, although the Boiler Room's relaxed atmosphere, pool table, and decent rock-oriented jukebox make it worth a visit. Mondays are $1 nights (domestic draft and well shots) if you're especially broke. My friend Jason, who has been coming to the Boiler Room since college, says that "it used to be the coolest, but now it's so bad it's good."

Perks: jukebox or DJ, pool, pinball, notebook full of takeout menus

Dive factor: 6

Historic Dives

Ear Inn
McSorley's
Ruby's
Rudy's
Bohemian Hall & Beer Garden

Botanica

212-343-7251
47 Houston Street, between Mott Street and Mulberry Street
Subway Directions: N/R to Prince Street, F/V/S to Broadway-Lafayette, 6 to Bleecker

Don't head to Botanica thinking it will live up to its name—no lush greenery here, folks. Still, it's the kind of dive that will have something for everyone in your crowd; it's artsy enough for your cool friends, cheap enough for your broke friends, and convenient enough for your lazy friends that don't like to travel to exotic locales far away from Houston Street. Maybe that's why the place is almost always too packed for my liking. One pal says his friend got a blowjob on a couch during the Saturday "rush hour" here without attracting any attention.

This prime site on Houston Street used to be the home of the old Knitting Factory, and Botanica really makes the most of the space. There's a smallish bar up front, tons of wooden table-and-chair sets and assorted thrift store couches in the front room, and a cool back room jam-packed with more mismatched furniture, which feels a bit like a '70s rec room in someone's basement, minus the shag carpet. It's a great place to cluster with groups. The ambiance is helped by dim lighting, groovy old chandeliers, a fake fireplace and other such "accents."

The bartenders can be chatty if need be, and they're usually dressed in the latest reveling finery (leather corsets, etc..) They also have cool mix tapes ready to go when the jukebox becomes tiresome.

When you've had enough of the smoke and loud conversations, be sure to pick up one of the cool Botanica postcards available on your way out to the street. And if you find Botanica too bridge-and-tunnel on Friday or Saturday nights, try it again on an off-night or an afternoon.

Perks: plenty of tables and couches, DJs

Dive factor: 4

Cherry Tavern

212-777-1448
441 E. 6th Street, between Avenue A and 1st Avenue
Subway Directions: F/V to Second Avenue, 6 to Astor Place

From what I can gather, there is only one reason to make multiple trips to the Cherry Tavern—the famous, infamous, and inebriating Tijuana Special—$4 for a can of Tecate and a shot of well tequila. However, those two words WELL TEQUILA probably won't sound so appealing the next morning.

The Cherry is a small, but not particularly homey, place. It's a great "meet here for a drink then figure out where to really go" joint, or a good place to bring in your "younger-looking" friends. It also tends to be quite empty during happy hour, so if you want to be sure of a seat, or really have to watch *Jeopardy*, this is your spot. At least the skinheads don't hang out here anymore.

The place is sparse—maybe 20 seats at the bar, along with two small tables. Bars on the windows lend a rather foreboding vibe, and prints of the infamous "Dogs Playing Poker" series don't add any more character. How much you enjoy the place may depend on whether you know any regulars, how many tattoos you have, or how comatose the bartenders are. Two of my former coworkers, good-looking guys, used to have no trouble picking up gals every time they came in. They even developed a sly code for when it was time for some Cherry Tavern cavorting: "It's time to pop into the cherry." One word of warning—if you decide to try and pop the cherry yourself, stick with the patrons. One friend of a friend got slapped—hard—when he admired a tattoo between the bartender's breasts.

Perks: pool, jukebox, the "Tijuana special," tattoos, popping in

Dive factor: 6

Cleo's 9th Ave Saloon

212-307-1503
656 Ninth Avenue, at 46th Street
Subway Directions: A/C/E to 42nd Street/Port Autority

If you're a clinically depressed gay man stuck between the theater district and Port Authority, this is the place for you. The crowd is comprised mostly of loners who seemed to be trying to cruise, but aren't aggressive enough to do much more than stare sadly into their cocktails.

My friend Chris and I ordered our usual Absolut and tonics and were a bit surprised they were $6 each, but that didn't really seem bad once we realized the drinks were sizeable and strong. Some mighty tasty free popcorn on the bar was a definite perk (hello, dinner!). The regulars seated around us seemed to be getting buybacks as you'd expect. (I had a chuckle when one regular ordered a cranberry *sauce* and vodka—remember that one next Thanksgiving.) Women don't seem overly welcome, but they aren't scorned.

Wednesday night karaoke may or may not liven things up. For the charity -minded, on Sundays the bar donates 50 cents from every drink to the charity God's Love We Deliver, so you can drink for a good cause! For the high culture set, there's some original artwork on the walls and some untouched books on a bookshelf up front.

The digital jukebox is a plus—a good mix from Bob Seger to ABBA to Sisqo's "Thong Song." If that's not enough entertainment for you, check out the front bulletin board with all kinds of posters for campy gay productions. My favorite was for the ballet spoof "Buttcracker."

Perks: digital jukebox, cigarette machine, ATM machine, bulletin board

Dive factor: 6

The Cock

212-777-6254
188 Avenue A, at 12th Street
Subway Directions: L to First Avenue, 6 to Astor Place

The Cock has only been open since 1998, but the place is already legendary as well as often packed. The tongue-in-cheek (no pun intended) name is furthered by the red neon rooster in the front window, but the place is actually as sexy and sleazy as its name suggests. From hipsters (singer Rufus Wainwright once rented the whole place for a photo shoot and party) to sleazers to that Starbucks guy you face every morning, every gay boy in town knows the Cock, or should.

On the hot night we visited, the $5 cover was definitely worth it to groove to a cool DJ, watch energetic go-go dancers on the bar, and lurk a bit in the back room (where, ahem, you can find some audience participation if that's what you're looking for). The air-conditioning wasn't pumping hard enough one summer night, but the sweaty vibe suited the place.

The Cock occasionally hosts theme nights and stage shows, although the now-legendary Foxy nights have been halted. (Customers would do anything outrageous to win Foxy's $100 prize—think enema and tampon tricks, huge turkey drumsticks pulled out of vaginas, pubic hair lit aflame, and lots of hand action.) Still, there's plenty to gawk at, or get involved with, at this one-of-a-kind bar. Even unofficial go-go boys can get in on the action—my friend Karl recently saw a go-go boy upstaged by a well-endowed patron who started trying for his own tips.

Don't bother showing up early—things don't get cocking, I mean cooking, 'til after midnight (do your pre-partying elsewhere). And if you're distracted by the hot men, heed those "watch your wallets" signs posted everywhere.

Perks: go-go dancers, DJs, theme nights, videos

Dive factor: 7

The Cock

Coyote Ugly

212-477-4431
153 First Avenue, between 9th and 10th Street
Subway Directions: F/V to Second Avenue, 6 to Astor Place, L to First Avenue
www.coyoteuglysaloon.com

Piper Perabo, what hath thou wrought? Sources tell me Coyote Ugly *was* a cool place when it opened in 1993, but now feels like a tourist attraction (and it is, with outposts in New Orleans, Las Vegas and Atlanta). In the movie named for this bar (based on a better *GQ* story by former bartender Elizabeth Gilbert) a gaggle of would-be stars work the bar, dancing their hearts out, looking to be "discovered." Sure enough, the real barmaids at this East Village haunt are still dancing away, but the only people here to discover them are scary bikers and Japanese tourists drooling at the bar.

The ladies are lovely and very scantily clad, but otherwise the place doesn't hold a lot of allure—think bras on the walls and smells of puke wafting through the air though the sun has barely set. A pal reports: "A bunch of depressing drunk chicks in ill-advised halter tops hoist themselves up on the bar to 'dance.' It's truly horrible." Voyeurs luck out occasionally—once two models shooting a Miller Lite ad started getting into one another and got naked, *not* for the ad campaign. And this before happy hour had started!

Coyote has a famous rivalry with the Village Idiot, whose original location across the street spawned this bar. I prefer the Idiot—it's less like a theme park of a dive bar, mostly due to the staff. Buxom ladies work both bars, but at Coyote they sound scripted when they try to be sassy, especially when saying the three rules of the bar—"We don't sell water, we don't sell pussy drinks, and don't piss on the seat." Even the bartop dances are choreographed, which takes a bit of the fun out of it. But it's not completely Disney-fied: tables *are* broken, Pat Benatar *is* blaring, and female patrons *are* encouraged to take off their bras, among other undergarments. Happy hour specials and cheap pitchers help you lose your inhibitions. You can also buy a souvenir T-shirt (I guess cans of Pabst don't travel well).

Perks: darts, jukebox, partial nudity

Dive factor: 7

Danny O's

No phone
5 Hyatt Street, at Stuyvesant Place, Staten Island
Travel Directions: Walk from the Staten Island Ferry Terminal

No offense to the fine inhabitants of Staten Island, but the best thing about this borough is the free ferry ride to and fro. The views are amazing, the benches comfy, and the food isn't as bad as you think ($2 hotdogs are the most popular offering). If you're viewing the ferry as a moving dive bar, be prepared to drink quickly—Bud tall boy cans are only $2.50, but the ferry ride is a quick 20 or so minutes, so chug while you can.

Lots of folks just ride the ferry straight back, but if you actually find yourself setting foot on S.I., there are a few ways to bide your time—most notably the cool Snug Harbor art gallery and gardens, the Staten Island Yankees baseball games, and, for yours truly, a few dive bars.

Danny O's is the most authentically divey bar I found within walking distance of the ferry terminal (there are other parts of Staten Island that are really lovely, but the bus system could be a real buzzkill after a few cheap beers). This little Irish dive's state of disarray—broken beer taps, broken bar stools, broken Waterworld pinball machine, broken toilet seat, one broken TV, one with bad reception, and a nearly broken front door—made my friend Michelle remark that it all must be a "work in progress." But I doubt any progress is planned.

The crowd was all male, Bud drinkers, working class, definitely born and raised on Staten Island, but they were friendly (even that one fellow that was missing most of his teeth) to us interlopers. The jukebox reflected the clientele—oldies, more Billy Ray Cyrus than should be allowed, Kenny Rogers, and something called *The Copulation Compilation*. But there were also some wild cards like a Partridge Family disc and Salt 'n' Pepa—throw on "Push It" and see how long it takes for the regulars to scowl at you.

Perks: cigarette machine, jukebox, TVs

Dive factor: 8

Desmond's

212-684-9472
433 Park Avenue South, between 28th and 29th Street
Subway Directions: N/R to 28th Street, 6 to 28th Street

Desmond's sticks out like a sore thumb on this stretch of rather swank, if generic, Park Avenue South. It provides a welcome alternative to the cavernous sports bar/restaurant Park Avenue Country Club, or a more low-key place to hang than squished in the bar for happy hour at Houston's. It also provides a bit of history—Desmond's opened in 1936 and actress Veronica Lake used to tend bar, a few years before The Who's Roger Daltrey became a regular.

The vibe isn't too flashy—it's a standard Irish pub with a bit of grime that attracts assorted sports enthusiasts (Mets fans and World Cup watchers) and your typical after-work suits. (And in this case, when I say suits, I'm thinking of IT guys with bad ties that look like Bobcat Goldthwait, not Michael Douglas in *Wall Street*.) On weekends the place fills up a bit as local bands play, but during the week there should be plenty of room to hit the bar, or the back tables, with your coworkers or friends. Typical pub food is served if you're hungry, and if you're thirsty early, note that the bar opens at 8 a.m.

The place isn't exactly uplifting, but I'm told that it has improved considerably in recent years—the OTB (Off-Track Betting) parlor that used to sit next door closed, so the floor of Desmond's is no longer littered with old OTB tickets or old OTB types. However, some of the old OTB spirit remains, as during one recent visit when an extremely inebriated gent offered the bartender $1000 to throw my drinking partner out of the bar. The patron then promptly threw up inches from my feet and was himself shown the door.

Perks: sells cigarettes and lifesavers, jukebox, TVs, occasional live music

Dive factor: 6

Best Sunday Afternoon Drinking

Freddy's
Blue & Gold
Barrows Pub
Bohemian Hall & Beer Garden
Ear Inn
Hank's Saloon

Dick's

212-475-2071
192 Second Avenue, at 12th Street
Subway Directions: L to Third Avenue, N/R/Q/W/4/5/6 to Union Square

This East Village institution is a great neighborhood gay dive, providing a welcoming place to warm up for a night out, or to have a no-frills nightcap on your way home. Dick's boasts a mix of neighborhood hipsters and older blue-collar fellows (both equally friendly). The décor is slightly '80s inspired (red lights pulsing inside plastic tubes), which can sometimes match customers' outfits (one chap was wearing a particularly retro-looking combo of cut-off jean shorts and sleeveless flannel plaid shirt).

A shopping cart hangs from the ceiling and plastic shower curtains cover the windows, though a recent renovation streamlined a portion of the junkyard ambiance. Blinds in the front—along with the dark interior—ensure that Dick's is nearly black even at high noon, always a good thing for a heavy boozer. The jukebox is a pleasing mix (dance tunes or the Magnetic Fields), and you may even encounter Stephen Merritt at the bar if you are lucky. Depending on when you drop by, you'll either find old musicals or porn on the TV sets. Sit back and order a famous Dick Shot—banana liqueur, butterscotch schnapps, and Bailey's. And tip well for your buybacks!

Perks: pool, jukebox, extra-dark lighting

Dive factor: 7

Doc Holliday's

212-979-0312
141 Avenue A, at 9th Street
Subway Directions: L to First Avenue, 6 to Astor Place

The first time I went to Doc Holliday's, I met some pals who had been there for about 2 hours. By the time I arrived, they had already built a "beer-amid" out of their empty Pabst cans on the table by the front window. Even passersby on the street were giving the thumbs up at their feat, and the funniest part was that my pals said they only got this bright idea after the first few rounds of cans had already been cleared away.

Doc Holliday's always strikes me as a good place to snag a table with a group of friends and drink as much as you want without anybody bothering you. The crowds, many looking to be straight out of college, mostly keep to themselves, although you might be able to mingle at the bar. (My pals Brooke and Mona once persuaded 15 strangers to shotgun beers with them.) Bartenders occasionally jump up on the bar to dance, and one friend of mine saw a particularly tall bartender hit her head on the ceiling. There is also the occasionl celebrity solo drinker, as one pal once spotted Jimmy Fallon doing shots by himself until closing time.

Lynyrd Skynryd's "Simple Man" is a staple on the jukebox, and it seems pretty apropos to Doc's, which is a pretty simple bar, adorned with TVs, steer horns, and video poker. The Western-themed mural on the outside of the building carries over to the interior—cowboy boots hang from the ceiling, and Texas and American flags adorn the walls alongside posters for old Westerns. Prices aren't as cheap as one might expect—we paid $9 for a Stoli and a bottle of domestic beer (with a strange hair stuck to the outside, no less). If that's too much for your wallet, try Tuesday nights for $7 all-you-can-drink draft. And do yourself a favor and go ahead and call in sick for Wednesday.

Perks: TVs, pool, video poker, jukebox

Dive factor: 6

Ear Inn

212-226-9060

326 Spring Street, between Hudson Street and Greenwich Street
Subway Directions: C/E to Spring Street, 1/2 to Canal Street

The Ear Inn is more of a neighborhood saloon/restaurant than a dive, but if you're in need of an unpretentious drink in this part of town (on the border of SoHo), or you can't get past the velvet rope at Sway across the street, this is your place. You'll have to fight for a stool at the bar most nights, but you can sit at a table and enjoy the rather fancy (and surprisingly affordable) food. Expect to rub elbows with musicians, transplanted foreigners, literary types and musicians. A lot of the patrons don't seem to be in the mood to mingle with strangers, but the few that are up for chatting can be quite engaging. (I had a good fight about my favorite band at the front bar one night.) On the nights when bands play it might be hard to have a quiet chat, so plan accordingly.

Even though I was hit on by a local restaurant owner while waiting in line for the ladies' room, women should feel comfortable going here alone—it's an upstanding place where you'll feel safe no matter what the hour (until you have to walk past the bikers outside). The amazingly cute bartender I spied one night doesn't hurt either.

The Ear Inn has quite a storied history—it's housed in an 1817 building called the James Brown House (not *that* James Brown) that was located on the edge of the Hudson River until landfill was added (the dusty bottles that decorate the area behind the bar look like they have been accumulating dirt for more than a century). The Ear was also a favorite of sailors and longshoremen, and some folks believe there are even a few ghosts lurking about. The bar's excellent name hints at its longevity—an old neon "BAR" sign with a damaged "B" translated into "EAR."

Perks: Live music, readings, food

Dive factor: 1

The Edge

212-477-2940
95 E. Third Street, between First and Second Avenue
Subway Directions: F/V to Second Avenue, 6 to Astor Place

My friend CJ, who has lived around the corner from The Edge for years, says this bar proves his "side street theory"—that you'll find a more local and laid-back crowd in bars on side streets than in those on main avenues. And laid-back is the best way to describe The Edge—there's even a sign on the door admonishing patrons to "sleep late." The place is spacious and rarely packed, which gives the laid-back locals plenty of room to spread out at the L-shaped bar, at clusters of couches and tables, or by the ever-popular pool table.

Don't let the exposed brick and cool art on the walls fool you, 'cause this place isn't as swank as it looks. Though the Hells Angels from next door don't come in here as often as they used to, there are still quite a few East Village barflies scattered about (wacky bisexuals, off-duty bartenders, and so forth). The manager also adds some spark—once when I was in the deli across the street buying beer for an apartment party, he was there buying limes and lemons and trying to lure folks from the deli to his bar.

You might as well sit back and enjoy the blaring tunes, 'cause the TV in here is at an awkward angle that would give you a neck cramp before the first inning's over.

Perks: pool, darts, jukebox

Dive factor: 2

Best Dives To Find a Date
(or a One-Night Stand)

Village Idiot
The Cock
Cherry Tavern
Motor City
Rudy's

Emerald Inn

212-799-0494
205 Colombus Avenue, at 69th Street
Subway Directions: 1/2/3 to 72nd Street, B/C to 72ne Street

This is a joint that might not be considered a dive on Avenue C, but on the Upper West Side you take what you can get. There's yellowing pictures of old men hanging behind the bar, and plenty of *actual* old men drinking in front of the bar. It's a pleasant spot to start your bar crawling, grab a few beers after the movies, or slum before hitting Lincoln Center. (It's not totally slumming, 'cause drinks aren't dirt cheap—pints are about $5.)

As you might have guessed from the name, the place is heavy on the Irish—comedian Denis Leary has been known to stop in for a green beer on St. Patrick's Day. The food served is passable, though the entrees were a bit salty and the mashed potatoes tasted instant. But it's real food, not just pretzels, and the menu does include a few Irish delicacies like Shepherd's Pie and Bangers & Mash. The menu touts that they are "Specialists in Irish Coffee," but I wasn't really in the mood to try a "Nutty Irishman."

Like any good Irish bar, the Emerald sports an extremely likable bartender and plenty regulars who stop in a few nights a week. The dingy décor is grimy-diner-meets-Irish-pub-meets-grandma's-house (check out the generic old paintings of a cornucopia and a river scene). Eat and booze at the bar or in the small diner-like red linoleum booths. If you've got a ménage à trois in mind, perhaps you'll want to ease into the topic at an adorable little bar shelf in the back, built for three. Vampiric day drinkers beware—there's a bright window at the front. Also beware the way-too-hot bathroom, which was cooking on a comfortable evening in June.

There's no jukebox, so you're at the mercy of whatever the bartender feels like playing—anything from oldies to Bob Marley to schlocky '80s hits. The place is fairly sedate, but a friend claims he once danced on the bar, so there are wild moments at the Emerald if you come at the right time.

Perks: full menu

Dive factor: 4

Frank's Cocktail Lounge

718-625-9339
660 Fulton Street, at South Elliot Place, Fort Greene, Brooklyn
Subway Directions: C to Lafayette Avenue, G to Fulton Street
www.frankscocktaillounge.com

At $5 for a bottled beer and a sometime-dance club upstairs, Frank's isn't the diviest place around. But this neighborhood joint in Fort Greene has so much damn character that I'd lose sleep if I didn't include it. The exterior has a great retro sign, complete with stylized martini glasses and the words "Frank's Cocktail Lounge." Don't be put off by the word "lounge"— we're not talking Soho style, we're talking old 70's funk (Frank's opened in 1974). The red and white color scheme gives the place a sultry vibe, which perfectly complements the frequent live jazz or R&B (former Hendrix sideman Lonnie Youngblood has a standing gig on Thursdays).

Let the young hipsters that are starting to populate the neighborhood take the side tables, and sit yourself down at the white stucco bar. It is here that you will hear great stories from old-timers, and sometimes from Frank himself. I got an earful of Atlantic City gambling tips one night from an old gent who'd lived in Fort Greene for decades. And, if you're ready to shake your groove thing, join the sweaty, grinning, and racially mixed masses towards the back. (Or perhaps the famed Friday night dance bash "Bang the Party" will return to Frank's?)

The only warning about Frank's is that the drink prices don't reflect the aging décor. But you're paying for ambience, and Frank's delivers. Why do you think Busta Rhymes filmed a video here?

Perks: DJs, live music, jukebox, dancing

Dive Factor: 4

Frank's Cocktail Lounge

Best Jukeboxes

Phoenix
O'Connor's
Siberia
Sweetwater

Freddy's

718-622-7035
458 Dean Street, at Sixth Avenue, Park Slope, Brooklyn
Subway Directions: 2/3 to Bergen Street, Q/2/3/4/5 to Atlantic Avenue

Freddy's would be cool even if it weren't the closest bar to my apartment. But since I can walk here in minutes, it holds a special place in my heart. A low-key establishment, going to Freddy's is like taking a day trip away from the city—the place is so darn welcoming. Although the crowd is usually a mix of neighborhood slackers and a few old men from the area, Freddy's winning ways are apparently attracting some new friends (we've spied some Manhattanites spending their Saturday nights here). All feel welcome, and there's much to love about this place—it's a spacious, beautiful old bar with friendly bartenders, polite patrons, and a well-behaved dog or two milling about. Cheaper beer than you'll find in Manhattan just adds to the good feeling.

If that's not enough for you, the back room boasts bands and readings several nights of the week (mostly weekends—check freddysbackroom.com for updates), plus rotating shows by emerging artists, some of whom have emerged more than others. There's also a pool table, and I recommend camping out by it during an off night—Sundays are my favorite—when you'll likely have most of the back room to yourself. (I once met Mike Tyson's assistant playing pool back there.) Literary types can dust off one of the aging hardcovers and read for a spell, or browse through back issues of the local 'zine *Lurch*.

My only complaint about Freddy's is that all the friendly (and hunky) firemen from the firehouse across the street don't come in enough!

Perks: back room with music and readings, dog-friendly, pool, TVs, jukebox, close to my apartment

Dive factor: 4

The Gardens

718-783-9335
493 Myrtle Avenue, at Hall Street, Clinton Hill, Brooklyn
Subway Directions: G to Classon Avenue or Clinton-Washington Avenues

Some might say that The Gardens is an oasis in this harsh half-ghetto/half-art student section of Brooklyn—but they would be wrong. Sure, there is a pleasing outdoor patio in the back, but the rest of this dismal bar is all dive. Though much of Clinton Hill is gentrifying, with plenty of signs for "lofts available" near the housing projects, this place hasn't spruced itself up for the newcomers.

My drink was shockingly expensive—$5.50 for a tiny (albeit strong) Absolut and tonic—maybe an okay price for Manhattan, but not for this part of Brooklyn. Evidently there are better deals available—like Bud drafts (12 oz.) for only a dollar from 4-6 p.m. (Yes, dollar drafts do still exist!)

The chief nod to interior décor seems to be the half-burned-out lights strung around the bar and the mirrors on the wall, that constantly remind you of the sad surroundings and sadder crowd (featuring, the night I was there, an octogenarian couple and a lone guy at the bar drinking a Coors Light over ice). If that's not unsettling enough, be aware that The Gardens is spying on you the whole time—a surveillance camera is perched near the door. The questionable clientele that hang in here late on weekend nights apparently aren't afraid of being seen on America's Most Wanted.

A more pleasant experience is available out back, in the "garden" that gives the bar its name. It's surprisingly pleasant out here—potted plants and trees, ivy-covered walls, and, when I was there, a professor from the nearby Pratt School of Art—even if the plastic tables have been tagged in graffiti and the malnourished cat looks like she could attack at any second.

Perks: TVs, pool, outdoor seating

Dive factor: 8

Grassroots Tavern

212-475-9443
20 St. Mark's Place, between Second and Third Avenue
Subway Directions: 6 to Astor Place, L to Third Avenue

It's a sweltering July day in the city, you don't have a share in the Hamptons, and you don't want to spend $10 on a heavily air-conditioned movie. What to do? Head to Grassroots Tavern, which in my unofficial estimate is the coldest bar in New York. The A/C is always pumping and the pitchers are always flowing, and that's enough to make it worth a trip to this oasis on annoyingly touristed St. Mark's Place. "The Root," as my pals Nik and Sara call their favorite hangout, is a perfect meet-up spot to start your evening's debauchery. You could even do their famous Boot and Root combo—a slice at nearby pizza restaurant Two Boots followed by a pitcher at the Root.

A long bar, plenty of draft beers, and loads of rustic wood tables will have you forgetting the summer, or winter, spring, or fall, in no time. Grassroots attracts a pleasingly mixed crowd of NYU students, office workers celebrating happy hour, aging frat boys in plaid shirts, a punk or two for good measure, and neighborhood old-timers who leave everyone else alone. It's not a mingly crowd, mostly couples and big groups, but there's some community atmosphere back by the dartboard. Even if you're not a regular, you can stop to say hello to the friendly (if lazy) dog and cat. The occasional tourists fit in, like the kilt-adorned Scotsmen who were celebrating with their pleather-outfitted newlywed friends. Note to self: do not marry anyone whose idea of a wedding reception is a pitcher of Bass on St. Mark's.

The upgraded jukebox features the usual mix of classic rock, Brit Invasion classics and requisite cheese—but also pleasant surprises like Motörhead, early Wilco, and the Stooges. Bathrooms leave a bit to be desired—the sink is airplane-sized and the toilet paper has been ingeniously made theft-proof by being looped with a big padlocked bike chain. But you're not here for the bathrooms, so stick to the bar and enjoy a basket of surprisingly tasty $1 popcorn. If you don't eat something, you'll see why Nik also calls the Root "the Puddlemaker": you walk in sober and walk out a puddle.

Dive Factor: 5

Perks: jukebox, dartboards, popcorn, air conditioning

Hank's Saloon

718-625-8003
46 Third Avenue, at Atlantic Avenue, Brooklyn
Subway Directions: Q/1/2/4/5 to Atlantic Avenue, M/N/R/W to Pacific Street
www.hankstavern.com

Before I actually entered Hank's, the place scared the hell out of me—mostly due to the old-timers I'd see loitering out front, the neon Schafer sign in the window, and the flames painted on the outside of the building. But inside, Hank's is fairly welcoming. The crowd definitely varies depending on when you visit—loads of bands play here, from neo-country to punk, and they bring their respective crowds with them. (Check the bar's website for an upcoming band calendar.) There are usually a few scary bikers and very old old-timers gathered at the bar, no matter what the scene. Usually the mismatched crowd mixes well, but on one Friday night, an old codger looked like he was ready to cry in his can of Pabst when a group of performance artists made some "music" while dressed as robots. Hard drinkers start their day when Hank's opens at 8 a.m. (noon on Sundays).

Hank's is a place where anybody can fit in. My friend Chris happened in there on a Sunday still wearing clothes (redneck T-shirt and acid washed jeans) from the previous night's White Trash party—nobody batted an eye.

Sundays at Hank's are a treat, with music and free BBQ that's tastier than the free hotdogs at Rudy's in Manhattan. Now that's hospitality.

Perks: jukebox, live music, free BBQ (Sundays)

Dive factor: 8

Hank's Saloon

Best for Groups

Parkside Lounge
Desmond's
Doc Holliday's
Vazac's 7B
Mare Chiaro
Bohemian Hall & Beer Garden

College Crowds

Alibi
Blue & Gold
Cherry Tavern
Holiday
Night Café

Hogs & Heifers

212-929-0655
859 Washington Street, at 13th Street
Subway Directions: A/C/E to 14th Street, L to 8th Avenue

212-722-8635
1843 First Avenue, between 95th and 96th Street
Subway Directions: 6 to 96th Street

I ask you this: would a real biker bar be hawking $30 T-shirts? When H&H opened in 1992, it probably *was* filled with real bikers and other assorted types (my friend Robert used to go there back then, and he called it Hogs and Heroin), but thanks to stories of Julia Roberts donating her bra to the bar's collection, the place is now crowded with tourists, Wall Streeters hoping to "slum it," and bachelorette parties of sorority girls looking for an authentic night out. I've even seen a group of Hasidic Jewish men in here taking in the scene, and that's certainly not what you expect at a biker bar. The gentrifying of the Meatpacking district doesn't help—you can pop in for a bite to eat at Pastis and then hit Hogs.

Still, H&H tries to be authentic. The infamous bartenders still pour shots, encourage bar dancing and shout through bullhorns. If you're tough enough, my friend Marisa recommends shouting back—she was the lone female patron here one lunch hour, and the bartender was berating her to dance on the bar. Marisa yelled back, "Fuck you bitch and pour the drinks!" winning the respect of the barkeep, the crowd, and her banker lunch date.

The music's still loud and the crowd is still hard-drinking (and on any given night you are likely to still see some "hogs" out front), so the place is definitely divey enough for me to recommend. However, I'd advise going on an "off" night like Monday or Tuesday, or during the day before the crowds get off work. Just watch your back—my friend Spesh may have been slipped a "mickey" one night (poor girl was puking for days). And beware—the crowd at the pool table is capital S-serious.

The uptown location is much the same, but features occasional live music, and a few less tourists venture that far north for their biker bar kicks. The downtown branch has a bit more of the "Girls Gone Wild" atmosphere.

Perks: pool, jukebox, bra collection, bar dancing

Dive factor: 7

Holiday Cocktail Lounge

212-777-9637

75 St. Mark's Place, between First and Second Avenue

Subway Directions: 6 to Astor Place, F/V to Second Avenue, L to First Avenue

Where is David Lynch's casting director when you need him? The Holiday Cocktail Lounge is perhaps the only bar where you can be served by a former Olympic athlete while listening to Kris Kristofferson on the jukebox. It is a one-of-a-kind, caught-in-a-time-warp bar that would seem more at home in a seafaring community than in the East Village. The beauty of this joint is its unchanging appearance—even the old bartender stays the same.

According to the informative plaque on the front wall (evidently someone was tired of telling the story to drunk customers over and over again), the bartender is named Steven Lutak, and he was born in 1920 in the Ukraine. He bought the bar (which has existed in several forms since 1936) in 1965, and over the years has attracted some famous patrons such as W.H. Auden and Shelley Winters (Trotsky used to live across the street, but no one's sure if he stirred up any trouble at the Holiday). Back in the day, the crowd was working class Italian and Ukranian, but today it seems to be either under 22 (it is very popular for the I-just-graduated-and-moved-to-New-York crowd) or over 50.

The front has a pleasing half-circle bar, which helps one to spy on (or chat with) your fellow patrons. But if you encounter single guys here with their noses tucked in books or playing chess, you might want to keep to yourself. The back section of the Holiday looks a bit like an old hometown pizza parlor, with hanging lights and a variety of tables and booths. The look is very "bar décor 101"—B&W TV so old it has a manual dial, a fake plant, nautical knick-knacks, and Busch and Schafer signs aplenty.

The bartender can be a bit crusty, but he gets friendlier (and much drunker) as the night goes on (he might get your order wrong, or better yet, forget to charge you). You may even catch the old guy crooning. Don't expect to stay here 'til the wee hours, though—the Holiday closes around 1. Also, there's no draft and the bottles selection is slim, just Bud, Amstel and Heineken. Beware the glaring bare bulb in the ultra-depressing bathroom—you're not as cute as you think!

Heed one warning—the drinks are potent (especially when the bartender is wasted). A pal of mine, admittedly not a hardened drinker, was here to celebrate quitting one job and starting another, but after two gin and tonics, she found her head down on the bar (and later found herself vomiting in a trashcan outside).

Perks: jukebox, cigarette machine

Dive factor: 7

Dives in Unexpected Places

Phil Hughes (Upper East Side)
Nancy Whiskey (Soho/Tribeca)
Milady's (Soho)
Barrows Pub (West Village)
Emerald Inn (Upper West Side)

Holland Bar

212-502-4609
532 Ninth Avenue, between 39th and 40th Streets
Subway Directions: A/C/E to 42nd Street/Port Authority

Amateurs take note! The Holland Bar prides itself on being a real drinker's bar, so you may have to engage in tolerance training before you even step in the door. The Hell's Kitchen location near Port Authority brings in a pleasing mix of clientele—old, young, working class, unemployed, you name it. Despite a somewhat intimidating look, the folks here are very friendly. Drinks are cheap ($3 pints or mixed drinks), but don't expect anything fancy—when we asked for Stoli, we were quickly informed that "we don't serve that here."

The décor has a lot of character (especially the cool old sign behind the bar, strung with Christmas lights), but the place itself doesn't have a lot of room—if you don't grab a seat at the skinny bar, there's barely anywhere to stand. All of which makes it easy to meet the fellow patrons, of course. One night my friend Beth and I met two guys who worked in the area and liked to stop in at lunch a few times a week (if you're boss is understanding, take note). Soon, they were giving us free songs on the jukebox and stirring up a pretty heady discussion about politics, racism and inner cities. Maybe we got all this attention because as females we were somewhat of a rarity in here—one of the guys quipped that it could be a gay bar because it's always full of men. (It's most certainly not, though.) And if the riffraff ever get too attentive, you can trust that the near-legendary bartender Dr. Bill will soon have them out on the street.

Perks: jukebox, Atomic Wings nearby if you get hungry

Dive factor: 8

Holland Bar

Howard Johnson's Times Square

212-354-1445
1551 Broadway, at 46th Street
Subway Directions: N/Q/R/S/W/1/2/3/7 to 42nd Street/Times Square

What could be worse than being elbow-to-elbow with lost tourists in Times Square? How about being stuck with lost tourists in this outpost of the legendary Howard Johnson's chain.

A sign outside, in trademark turquoise and orange, beckons customers in for "a decanter of Manhattan, Martini or Daiquiri." The 4-7 p.m. happy hour at HoJo's is a real steal—all drinks (except premium brands) are $3.25. Plus, if you're really poor, you can take advantage of the free happy hour chow (edible but not-too-gourmet selections like dried-out pasta and egg salad sandwiches). Other than that, there is no reason to be here, as the food looks like TV dinners and the carpet is dirty. After happy hour, bottles of Bud will run you $4.50 and tiny mixed drinks start at $5.50. And, you have to put up with horribly bright lights and the sound of crashing dishes in the kitchen by the bar.

If you do venture in, keep the drink orders simple because the bartenders are novices—one young lady who couldn't even operate a corkscrew had a cheat sheet on the cash register that included the recipe for a Long Island Iced Tea.

As a New Yorker, there are only two reasons you'd venture in here: the cheap happy hour or a desire to feel like a suburbanite stuck in the '70s.

Perks: food (if you want to risk it), free buffet at happy hour, the orange booths!

Dive factor: 7

Most Men

Baby Doll Lounge
Alibi
Subway Inn
Mona's
Nancy Whiskey

International Bar

212-777-9244
120 1/2 First Avenue, beteween 6th and 7th Street
Subway Directions: F/V to Second Avenue, 6 to Astor Place L to First Avenue

A good reason not to judge a bar by it's name—the International is no jet-setting Eurotrash lounge, but a slightly filthy place to settle in and down eons of $3 bottles of Bud. If you are not careful, you may miss it—I walked by it for years without venturing in due to the narrow nondescript store-front. Inside, the place is homey and full of character, with a long bar up front, some tables in back that look like rejects from an ice cream parlor, and decorations that include upside down Christmas trees attached to the ceiling (it looks cooler than it sounds), inflatable globes, plastic skulls and bones, a year-round Happy New Year sign, and a condom box taped to the mirror behind the bar.

The bartenders are friendly even if you're not a regular, and the crowd is also quite pleasant—and because of the narrow bar space, you'll make friends whether you like it or not. The bathrooms are very small (definitely not a place for group action), and you'll have to wash your hands at an unbelievably small sink stuck amongst the tables in the back. Further back, the cement "patio" is not really much of a draw.

There's no draft, but plenty of cheap bottles, and as my friend Charles noted, the beers are so cheap that it's like "an all you can eat buffet." Mixed drinks are small but stiff. The jukebox, with an elk head on top and a "play at your own risk" sign, has a pleasing mix that goes beyond the usual standards—Ramones, Hank Williams, Rolling Stones, Run-DMC.

FYI, an Iowa Writers Workshop grad told a friend that "all the poets in Manhattan hang out in here," if that kind of thing is a draw to you. Perhaps the poets draw inspiration from the old Polish dude fond of telling stories about how when he was a baby he was held by Paul Robeson and Charles de Gaulle.

Perks: outdoor patio, it's always Christmas (if you hang upside down)

Dive factor: 6

Jackie's Fifth Amendment

No phone
404 Fifth Avenue, at 7th Street, Park Slope, Brooklyn
Subway Directions: F/M/N/R to Fourth Avenue/9th Street

When a friend and I visited Jackie's on a wintry Monday night, we were the only folks in the place under 40. I quickly picked up an important tip from the old- timers gathered at the long bar—buckets are essential. You see, upon first entering, I had just ordered a beer, and got a wimpy 7 oz. Pony bottle for $2.50. Then I noticed that the seasoned pros around me all had plastic buckets on the bar in front of them; soon I too had a bucket of my own—five pony bottles of beer (Bud, Bud Light, Coors Light and MGD are available)—for only $6! A bargain that makes the trip to Jackie's worth the trek.

Jackie's is a neighborhood joint that has been around the fringes of Park Slope since long before hipster bars like Loki Lounge or Great Lakes opened down the street (Jackie's has more character than those places anyway). And Jackie herself is indeed behind the bar, welcoming and sweet, even if she didn't want to discuss the bar's history in any depth with us.

The evening we were there, the TVs were tuned to "Jeopardy" and the regulars were palling around with one another—at times their conversation had the boisterous tones of a family feud, but it was all in good fun. The jukebox has a strange mix of songs, with schlock like Mariah Carey and Celine Dion alongside Hank Williams, Jr., Olivia Newton John and Britney Spears. I was pleased, however, to find some soft rock gems among the collection – Barry Manilow and the Doobie Brothers made a nice soundtrack to accompany our buckets of beer.

Perks: soft rock classics on the jukebox, TVs, buckets of beer!

Dive factor: 8

Jeremy's Ale House

212-964-3537
254 Front Street, at Dover Street
Subway Directions: 4/5/6 to Brooklyn Bridge/City Hall

It's located near the Fulton Fish Market (mmmm . . . the aroma!), yet Jeremy's Ale House doesn't discriminate against landlubbers. If you really want to be a regular, try the 8 a.m. happy hour that attracts die-hard fishermen and cops getting off the overnight shift. For those of us who prefer to drink after the sun sets, Jeremy's shares a secret it must have learned from its Fulton Fish Market neighbors. You see, fish is kept fresh and cold in Styrofoam containers, and Jeremy's also offers beer in huge 32 oz. Styrofoam cups, a bargain at six bucks (for the less lushy, there are normal pints available). Mixed drinks don't get Styrofoam, but they do get served in eye-poppingly huge plastic cups.

On the whole, the crowd is not particularly refined, but is the perfect group to accompany a few beers or some fried clams. In the summer, the place is packed with downtown types enjoying those big drinks, the tasty seafood and the concrete patio to the side of the main bar. Even when it's packed, Jeremy's doesn't feel claustrophobic because the bar is so damn cavernous. A former garage for trucks, the place features extremely high ceilings (you can see bras and clipped neckties from past patrons all around). It's less crowded in the off-season, although sports fans flood the place to watch big games.

The bar still attracts some old-timer fishmongers—Jeremy's opened as a seaport concession stand in 1974 and later moved to these larger digs. Because of the large drinks and the sea air, sometimes the rules of the land can be forgotten. When I was there, two amorous patrons tried to put on a public sex show in a corner of the bar. Management put an end to that one, despite protests from shocked onlookers.

Perks: TVs, outdoor space, famous calamari

Dive factor: 4

Jimmy's Corner

212-221-9510
140 W. 44th Street, between Broadway and Sixth Avenue
*Subway Directions: N/Q/R/S/W/1/2/3/7 to Times Square/42nd Street,
B/D/F/V to 42nd Street*

Jimmy's is a real find amidst the theater district tourist traps and cheesy bars of Times Square. This nearly 30-year-old bar is full of old-time New York character (rumor has it that some scenes of *Raging Bull* were shot here), from its décor—mostly boxing memorabilia—to its jazz-laden jukebox. The patrons are a great mix of construction workers, *New Yorker* editorial staffers, and Jimmy himself—boxing trainer and gym owner Jimmy Glenn. Photos of the greats adorn nearly every inch of the walls—check out great shots of Ali, Tyson, Holyfield and many lesser-known names.

If there's a pay-per-view fight, the place will be elbow-to-elbow. Come to think of it, the place is usually elbow-to-elbow anyway, thanks to the incredibly narrow front bar. For more room, head towards the back, where you'll find small tables and friendly waitress service. Drinks are small but strong, and where else in midtown are you gonna find a cool place to sit with a $3.50 cocktail while listening to the Captain and Tennille's "Love Will Keep Us Together?" Free baskets of pretzels are available on request, too!

Perks: boxing experts on call, jukebox, waitress service

Dive factor: 4

Narrowest Bars
(For Better Mingling!)

International Bar
Blarney Cove
Johnny's
Milano
Jimmy's Corner
Mars

Joe's Bar

212-473-9093
520 E. 6th Street, between Avenues A and B
Subway Directions: 6 to Astor Place, F/V to Second Avenue, L to First Avenue

I was introduced to the place by my good pals Michelle and John, who lived just a few blocks away for many years and counted themselves as semi-regulars. Not to be confused with the swank Joe's Pub near Astor Place, Joe's Bar is a little-known watering hole in Alphabet City whose main features are dilapidated chairs, flocked velvet wallpaper, and a healthy dose of personality. Whether you encounter the North Carolina businessman inviting you to his "river party," the retired Army folk, the sweet Polish bartender or groups of the tattooed rocker set, you're sure to find someone in this joint that fits your definition of "character." Maybe that's why Janeane Garafalo and writer Sebastian Junger have been spotted at the bar. One pal of mine found himself swing-dancing with strangers on Elvis's birthday, and where else in New York could you do that? (Assuming you would want to.)

The other draws of Joe's are the stiff competition on the pool table (unskilled amateurs stay away), and a complete lack of pretension (exhibit A: they sell beef jerky!). Draft beer comes in small mugs, which aren't quite large enough for my pint-swilling self (stick to the cheap bottles instead). The jukebox is mostly country, with legends like Waylon and Willie alongside newcomers such as the fabulous Laura Cantrell, but the crowd is typically a bit more punk rock. Just steer clear of the pickled eggs for sale behind the counter.

Perks: pool, classic country jukebox

Dive factor: 5

Johnny's Bar

212-741-5279
90 Greenwich Avenue, between 12th and 13th Streets
Subway Directions: 1/2/3 to 14th Street, A/C/E to 14th Street

For such a hole in the wall, Johnny's holds a special significance for quite a few people connected to this book (and it made a lovely cover photo). For me, it became the unofficial living room for an *insanely* small studio apartment that I lived in for a year across the street. It's also where my friend Beth and I spent many hours discovering our shared affections for dive bars, jukeboxes, and flirting. Later, Beth met the love of her life, Robert, when their mutual friend, the bartender/owner Peter introduced them. Turns out that Robert and his pals Rusel and Johnny had spent hours in Johnny's plotting the launch of their small press, so six degrees of Johnny's later, here's my book, through the help of their press. (And Beth and Robert are now married, despite starting their relationship with a drunken one-night stand sparked at Johnny's).

Enough about the Kevin Baconesque connections and more about the place itself. The current incarnation of Johnny's, named after an old neighborhood fixture who used to live upstairs, has been around since 1990. Before that, it existed for decades as Jack Barry's, and its theater-patron owner attracted drinkers like Robert Duvall and assorted musicians and barkeeps (including Jason Robards and Jessica Lange).

Physically, the bar is fairly nondescript—Johnny's is tiny, long and skinny, with Christmas lights on the brick walls, a few bar stools gathered around the stretched-out bar, a tiny but decent wall-mounted jukebox, and two airplane bathroom-sized restrooms in the back. So why do we all love this place so? It's the people, stupid. Johnny's is one of the few places in this rather posh West Village where you are sure to still encounter authentic, old-fashioned, pre-Guiliani-type New York barflies. Some of my favorite run-ins (in no particular order): the Swiss jazz musicians I met one New Year's Eve, the *New York Observer* writer and his prep school buddies on hallucinogens, the New Zealander who wanted to schedule a drink date (but said it was easier to reach him at another bar across town than at his home phone), the guy who was flipped out by doors because he got stuck in an elevator for the entire weekend, the guy who invited me and a pal back to his place late-night to "break some shit," the poet who worked in a subway booth, the guy who'd been knighted in England but may have been incarcerated at one point or another, and of course the guy who told me all about shooting his brother's pit bull. It may be a scary list, but there are normal neighborhood regulars such as accountants and movie theater managers in here as well. So pull up a stool, grab a pint and decide if you'd like your conversation sane or insane—Johnny's is sure to delight no matter what you're seeking. And don't be surprised if you've got the ultra-friendly bartenders, including the owner, Peter, talking to you like an old pal in no time.

Perks: jukebox, TV, buy-two-get-one-free from noon to 3 p.m., individuals of varying levels of sanity, great matchbooks that read "Who Do You Know That Needs A Drink?"

Dive factor: 6

Avoid On Saturday Night

Coyote Ugly
Cherry Tavern
Hogs & Heifers
Sophie's

Johnny's Famous Reef

718-885-2086
2 City Island Avenue, City Island, Bronx
Subway Directions: 6 to Pelham Bay Park, then Bx29 City Island Bus

Technically, this is more a restaurant than a bar, but it's open until 2 on Friday and Saturday, they have awesome frozen drinks, $2 cans of beer, and a huge outdoor patio on the water, so what the hell, I'll recommend it anyway.

There are plenty of fish shacks on City Island (and not much else), but Johnny's is old and authentic (it opened in 1954) and also on the very tip of the island, which gives its concrete patio a perfect view of the water. It is almost always packed with Bronx families and other city folks who need a dose of the nautical life but are too poor to hit the Hamptons. The first time I came here,with my parents no less, I spotted a regular from another dive bar I frequent.

You can eat typical trashy beach food like hot dogs or pizza, but the seafood is where it's at—steamed or fried fish, shrimp, oysters, clams, lobster tails, even frog legs. The food is no-frills but tasty, served cafeteria style in little paper baskets. Skip the depressing indoor wasteland of tables and head outside to the patio (slightly less depressing, with the quaint vibe of a prison yard), where the seagulls stalk you and whatever is rotting next door. Still, once you've had some fish and a few drinks, you can sit back and dream that you are miles away from NYC (those $2 beers will help).

If you're looking for more fun after chowing at Johnny's, try the City Pub, where locals warned us that the only patrons were three-toothed men, or Rhodes, where my posse and I spent a boozy Saturday night doing karaoke with the locals.

Getting to the quaint enclave of City Island by car is easy, but is more of an adventure by public transportation. Avoid the place in wintertime because Johnny's, like most of City Island, is open only from March to November.

Perks: food, outdoor patio

Dive factor: 3

Karavas Place

212-243-8007
164 W. Fourth Street, at Cornelia Street
Subway Directions: A/C/E/F/V/S to West 4th Street

West Village hangout Karavas is mostly known as a quick place to get some of the best and cheapest Greek food in New York City outside of Astoria, but there's a plain bar in the back where you can settle in for a few comfortable, if nondescript, hours of drinking. Drinks are fairly cheap, and there's a hefty selection of 11 beers on tap, from Coors Light to Hoegaarden. The crowd is mostly unhip and middle-aged, although one bartender, an aspiring fashion designer from London, adds some coolness. The jukebox isn't the best around, but it boasts both Ryan *and* Bryan Adams, along with "Rico Suave" and other novelties. If you're ready to work off your souvlaki, the downstairs area is open on weekends, where you can belt out a karaoke tune or groove to a DJ.

Karavas doesn't offer much in the way of décor, just rows of wooden booths, some dusty antique Pepsi bottles, and two vintage guns behind the bar (let's hope they stay there). No matter how much Ouzo you down, you won't be transported to the Greek Isles—there's a wall of windows that constantly remind you of the masses swirling around the heart of the Village.

Perks: jukebox, downstairs lounge, video games, Greek food

Dive factor: 2

Scariest dives

Mars
Billymark's West
Walter's
Spinning Wheel
Blarney Cove

Leisure Time Bowling Center

212-268-6909
625 Eighth Avenue, at 40th Street, Port Authority Bus Center, Upstairs
Subway Directions: A/C/E to 42nd Street/Port Authority

Looking for a way to pass the time that is even more pathetic than bowling in the bowels of Port Authority? Try drinking with the non-bowlers hanging out at the bowling alley's bar. Physically, there's nothing distinguishing about the surroundings—plenty of sports photos adorn the walls, and the big screen TVs, rows of booths and pitchers of beer make this a fine place to catch the big game. That is, if you can stomach the Celine Dion on the jukebox, the horrid turquoise and red color scheme, and the hilarious floor-shaking rumble of the Port Authority buses nearby. But after a couple of brews, if you get the urge to knock down some pins or hit the arcade, you're in the right place.

However, what makes the Leisure Time Bowling Center bar the place *not* to be is the clientele. Within a 10 minute period one night, my friend Beth and I witnessed a man in a Bugs Bunny shirt trying to start a fight with another patron, an obviously culinary-inclined fellow enjoying the free Swedish meatballs and drinking Bud Ice, and, if that weren't enough, we were then propositioned for a threesome by a seemingly upwardly mobile employee from the Port Authority's Duane Reade drugstore. We politely decided his offer, but you gotta give a man props for saying what's on his mind, no?

Perks: plenty of TV, occasional free snacks, food, bowling, ménage à trois offers, arcade

Dive factor: 4

Library

212-375-1352
7 Avenue A, between 1st and 2nd Street
Subway Directions: F/V to Second Avenue, 6 to Astor Plce, L to First Avenue
www.librarybarnyc.com

The Library is more of a neighborhood hangout than a tried and true dive bar, but it met three "dive qualifications", so it made the cut:

1) It's insanely dark (good for canoodling or hiding an ugly blind date).
2) The blaring jukebox completely kicks ass—Buzzcocks, Pixies, Motorhead, Replacements, and other 70s/80s/90s gems.
3) There's a 2-for-1 happy hour from 5 to 8—much better than a wimpy $1-off happy hour.

Though they host the occasional film screening, the Library is generally known for round-the-clock showings of kung-fu movies and other assorted schlock (the original *King Kong* is a favorite), which are projected onto a screen on the back wall. As far as frills, that is pretty much it. Mostly, the Library is about cheap drinks and loud music (don't bother going here to have a quiet conversation). It's also a great place for small birthday parties, because it never gets jam-packed. And if your parents, or your boss or significant other, whom you want to get away from for a night ask you where you're going, you can honestly tell them you are "going to the Library." The walls are in fact covered with books, but I've never seen a single person reading in here.

Perks: great jukebox, happy hour, pinball, takeout available from Nice Guy Eddie's next door

Dive factor: 3

Most Women

Ear Inn
119
Three of Cups
Village Idiot
Blue & Gold

Lucy's

No Phone
135 Avenue A, between St. Mark's and 9th Street
Subway Directions: L to First Avenue, F/V to Second Avenue, 6 to Astor Place

Lucy's has always represented something of a conundrum for me. I've been there literally dozens of times over the past five or six years, yet I cannot say I've ever had a *great* time. Still, I never protest the idea of venturing in. Perhaps it's the dirt-cheap drinks and the ultra-convenient locale that keeps the crowds coming back to Lucy's. It can be the perfect spot for a pre-party meet up or before heading to somewhere a bit more interesting in the East Village. (Be very distrustful of a local who's never thrown back a few at this old standby.)

Lucy's is a small, dingy place, but most times it's bearably packed—you can usually score one of the old dinette-style tables on the side of the bar. The crowd mostly gathers around the two always-busy pool tables in the back (known as the big one and the little one—one's regulation size and one isn't); there's usually not a lot of mingling by the bar. Assorted hipsters and old-timers take advantage of the video and pinball games. My pals Thom and Brooke once spent a full hour amusing themselves with a pornographic video version of "What's Wrong With This Picture?"

Lucy's has no doubt seen some hard times because of its proximity to Tompkins Square Park—a hand-lettered "NO DRUGS" sign hangs near the cash register. But the crowd doesn't seem terribly dangerous now (nor does the park). Occasional appearances by Lucy herself, or her daughter, add some needed character to the joint.

Perks: two pool tables, video games, jukebox

Dive factor: 8

Lys Mykyta (Sly Fox)

212-673-6479

140 Second Avenue, between St. Mark's and 9th Street

Subway Directions: F/V to Second Avenue, 6 to Astor Place

In addition to a damn cool name (taken from a Ukrainian folk tale), the Sly Fox is refreshingly free of pretense. You can buy strong and cheap beers, talk to the regulars, and enjoy free popcorn (don't expect any fancy-schmancy popcorn machine—we're talking Act II microwave popcorn that's lukewarm and slimy with fake butter).

Lys Mykyta is housed in the Ukrainian National Home, which means that on any given night you might stumble into a crowd of touring Ukrainian singers, dancers or other performers. Likewise, the décor is Old World meets Spencer Gifts—the booths up front are separated by weird iron gates and there is a bowling trophy along with weird purple lights behind the bar. It's way too bright up front near the jukebox. However, the crowd that gathers here doesn't seem to mind—it's mostly comprised of scary locals who aren't afraid to slam a shot glass on the bar to get the bartender's attention, people too drunk to know where they are (like the couple seated near me who were licking each other's necks), or very young college types. The guy who walks from spot to spot desperately trying to sell flowers should take note that he's not likely to get much business in the Sly Fox; it's definitely not the most romantic spot (despite the neck lickers). The jukebox reflects that—faves are AC/DC, Ozzy Osbourne's "Crazy Train," or Quiet Riot. One other important item to know—the bathroom situation is confusing, so ask the friendly bartender how to get there.

The Sly Fox is a great place to use if you want to play a practical joke on unsuspecting friends. My friend Dave once pulled a Sly and Foxy by sending online invitations to a group of people inviting them to a supposedly "swank" party at a new place called the Sly Fox. He reported that only a dozen people showed up, laughed heartily, and left immediately.

Perks: jukebox, TVs, popcorn

Dive factor: 7

Mare Chiaro

212-226-9345
176 1/2 Mulberry Street, between Broome and Grand Street
*Subway Directions: J/M/N/Q/R/Q/Z/6 to Canal Street, S to Grand
Street, J/M to Bowery*

My friend Melissa stumbled upon this place one night soon after she moved to New York, and she immediately fell in love with the Sinatra-heavy jukebox and the sawdust-laden floor. She quickly brought all her pals to visit the place she called "the Cosi Nostra bar.." While we've never run into Sammy the Bull or his pals at Mare Chiaro, the place does have a very old Italian feel. As a matter of fact, this little joint has so much Little Italy authenticity that scenes from *Donnie Brasco* and one of *The Godfather* sequels have been shot here, along with count-less magazine photo shoots. The place isn't Italian through-and-through, though, as Asian bartenders serve up the cheap bottled beers.

Unfortunately the Little Italy locale means you might be annoyed sev-eral times by folks trying to sell flowers to tourists. The crowd is a fun mix of hipsters, old-timers and tourists who've just eaten overpriced plates of linguini in Little Italy's scores of restaurants. The place is usually either packed or completely deserted—count yourself lucky if one of the Formica tables is available. If you get there early enough to claim some table space, Mare Chiaro is a great place to take a group, especially a group of out-of-towners looking for a slice of old New York. Be warned: your late-night plans to strike up a conversation with the interesting-looking owner Tony, who gives the place the nick-name "Tony's Nut House," might not go over so well. So just sit back and enjoy the pre-"Nolita" vibe, the authentic tin ceilings, and the opera and crooning on the jukebox.

Perks: oldies-heavy jukebox, historic sawdust

Dive factor: 6

Mars Bar

No Phone
25 E. First Street, at Second Avenue
Subway Directions: F/V to Second Avenue

I met my first Mars Bar regular half a world away, at a dive bar in Barcelona
where we shared shots of absinthe and some local hash. He was a musician from Red Hook, Brooklyn on a tour of Europe, and he suggested I
check out the Mars when I returned stateside. I regret that I only recently
took him up on his advice. The Mars has a reputation as possibly the seedi-
est bar in town, with whispers of heroin addicts lining up in the bathrooms and whatnot. My pal Mark, a die-hard fan of dives, said he'd never
dare to touch his hands to anything inside the Mars, much less touch his
lips to a drink here.

When I actually ventured inside, I saw only one person who was looked
like a smackhead, and everybody else was quite friendly. There was a news-
paperman, an artist, two men covered in tattoos talking about non-profit
grant applications, and even a dude in Birkenstocks. As a matter of fact,
two separate people approached our group and told us we looked familiar
even though none of us had ever been there before. Evidently, this is the
sort of place where everybody almost knows your name—like *Cheers* if
Norm was a less functional alcoholic. Like the motto on the wall says, this
is "day care for drunks."

Despite the friendly crowd, the Mars Bar more than lives up to its reputation as New York's King (and Queen and Prince) of dives. If you're up for
adventure, you might find it here, wrapped in many layers of filth. The
place is dank, dark and dirty, and the night I was there I saw the largest
cockroach I have ever seen in New York City. In addition, the bathrooms
will put fear in the hearts of mere mortals. It also worried me a teensy bit
that the obviously intoxicated bartender (obvious because she was drinking shots) was mixing drinks with orange juice sitting out behind the bar
like you'd see at some frat party. (Perhaps the health department should
be concerned). But the drinks are stiff enough that any botulism concerns
fall by the wayside. They are also cheap—$9.50 for a Stoli, a Stella and a
Rolling Rock.

Though the Mars gets this book's one and only "10" for diviness, it does

Mars Bar

have a cool, eclectic interior. If you dare to enter, notice the outsider art paintings, mismatched office chairs, weird bar carvings and graffiti (spotted on the ceiling: "L'Etat C'est Moi," The State Is Me), and glass bricks that reminded me of my orthodontist's office from the '80s. The crowning touch, however, are the cases of beer stacked up in the back like the Great Wall of China, plus dozens upon dozens of empties strewn about the rest of the bar. If all of this isn't enough to leave your head spinning with wonder at what the seedy years of pre-Guiliani NYC were like, you're assured of at least a bit of a time warp thanks to an old alarm clock that always reads "Wed Jan 23."

Perks: peanut machines, jukebox (from punk to doowop), pinball

Dive factor: 10

McSorley's Old Ale House

212-473-9148

15 E. 7th Street, between Second and Third Avenue

Subway Directions: F/V to Second Avenue, 6 to Astor Place, L to Third Avenue

Some purists will balk at my inclusion of McSorley's in a list of dive bars— the place is more historic than divey, having opened in 1854. But you can still get $2 mugs of beer (and you can't buy just one—good motto), there's sawdust on the floor, there's an occasional tourist puking outside, and they actually sell onions and crackers. So the place isn't exactly the Ritz (pardon the pun).

I'll start by confessing my family's fondness for McSorley's—my grandfather's cousin, a writer named Joseph Mitchell, helped to make the place famous with his 1950s *New Yorker* essay "McSorley's Wonderful Salon," later published in book form. (I recommend reading his whole anthology, *Up In the Old Hotel*—no, I'm not getting any royalties, but reading it will make you a better person.)

Having said that, I rarely venture into McSorley's anymore because it's usually far too crowded with white-hatted frat boys and tourists. But I have had some good times here, especially when I started off early in the afternoon when you can find a seat. One saving grace is that the crowds here are usually overly friendly (even if the barstaff isn't) and the communal tables ensure that you will have a buddy or two (or ten) in no time.

Because of its long and colorful history, McSorley's is a bar full of stories. The two that I have concern my pals Kathie, who almost fell on top of actress Martha Plimpton when she was trying to leave through an emergency exit, and Richard, who witnessed one drunken guy grabbing an elderly Asian gentleman while screaming "I'm hugging a Chinese man!"

Despite its popularity, McSorley's can still be a pleasant place to spend some time, particularly in the afternoon. So choose the house brew in light or dark, get a plate of sliced onions served with saltines, and settle in for awhile until the crowds arrive (the back room tends to be a bit homier). For entertainment, you can watch the waiters deftly juggle dozens and

McSorley's Old Ale House

dozens of beer mugs with their bare hands. And feminists take note—a tiny bit of good-old-boy attitude still survives here, since they didn't start letting female patrons in until 1970, when a court ordered them to.

Perks: history, food, TVs, I'm sort of indirectly related to the bar

Dive factor: 3

Milady's

212-226-9340
162 Spring Street
Subway Directions: C/E to Spring Street

In most places in America, Milady's would be an above-average neighborhood bar. But it happens to be situated smack in the middle of hipperthan-thou Soho, so it qualifies as a dive bar because of its location. If you're looking to cool your heels after a hard day at the Prada store, you might not feel quite comfortable in this unassuming spot, but otherwise this place will appeal to all crowds. I've spied blue-collar workers sitting next to Soho neighbors who came in for a few brews while walking the dogs. I also once spotted Jarvis Cocker (the lead singer of English art-rockers Pulp), who was being totally ignored by the masses except for one overzealous and over-inebriated fan (OK, OK, it was me). Bruce Springsteen also pops in from time to time.

Milady's is cleaner than your average dive, so you don't have to fear the food they serve. But drinks are the main course—there's a good beer selection and the usual liquors are available. The bar is friendly and mingly, especially when it is crowded (as it tends to be on weekend nights), and the tables are pretty cozy.

Milady's is the perfect spot to find affordable enough drinks and sit for hours catching up with friends. One memorable night here I even made a pact to move to Australia with my best pals—Spesh and Melis. We haven't made it there *yet*, but we have made many return visits to Milady's.

Perks: pool, food served, jukebox, dog-friendly

Dive factor: 2

Milady's

Milano's

212-226-8632
51 Houston Street, between Mott and Mulberry Streets
Subway Directions: N/R to Prince Street, 6 to Bleeker Street, F/V/S to Broadway-Lafayette

Milano's has been serving the heavy drinkers on the border of Little Italy since 1880, and it has all the hardboiled character of a hundred-plus-years old establishment. Unlike Botanica a few doors down, Milano's isn't filled with thrift-store attired hipsters nodding their heads to old Pavement albums. The clientele here is a mix of old-timers, laid-off dot-commers, a smattering of tourists, and workers (blue and white collar) grabbing a drink after work. This semi-hardcore mixture gives the place a surly and smoky vibe, but there are generally a few friendly faces amongst the barstools and the Irish bartenders.

The physical space reflects its nineteenth-century heritage—tin ceiling, tile floor, swinging saloon doors on the restrooms. When you enter the place (or try to walk toward the back) you have to brush up against every person seated at the bar, due to the excessively small amount of room (think of it as running the gauntlet of heavy drinkers). The walls are adorned with photo collages of patrons past and present, many blurry due to the work of an obviously drunken cameraman. You'll also find plenty of Sinatra memorabilia covered in a layer of grime, along with a large plastic bottle of Moet hanging from the ceiling. The jukebox is filled with Irish jigs, Sinatra, Johnny Cash, U2 and Simon and Garfunkel, although we did manage to get funky and place some ABBA on a recent visit.

Milano's doesn't cater to the champagne crowd, but if you order a Bud and settle into a barstool or one of the tables in the back, you'll easily fit right in and forget what time of day it is (like everyone else in the bar).

Perks: TVs, jukebox, potato chips for sale at bar

Dive factor: 7

Mona's

212-353-3780
224 Avenue B, between 13th and 14th Streets
Subway Directions: L to First Avenue

Mona's vibe, as my friend David remarked, "isn't exactly a party." It's not that the folks here aren't friendly, it's just that you may not be looking for these kinds of friends. On one of our nights here, we were surrounded at the bar by (in no particular order): a guy muttering to himself for HOURS, another guy who told us about his partially paralyzed ex-girlfriend (she had been hit by a car one night when they were coming home from Sophie's), and a third gentlemen who threatened to blow up his friend's house. Now that's a fiesta!

To be fair, Mona's does have some things going for it—for the ladies, it has tons of men. For the men, it has lots of guys to talk sports with, particularly European football. The pool games in the back can be quite serious, but up front things are a bit more lively, helped along by more cutting edge music, from punk to trip-hop, than you'd expect in a dive. Free-flowing pints and pitchers (ours of Bass was only $14, with domestics much cheaper) can really help the ambiance. For hearty drinkers, Thursday brings $2.75 pints of Guinness all day. If you don't get lucky with the human patrons, there are always friendly dogs milling about.

The place is harshly dark, so they don't take kindly when lost bridge-and-tunnel girls stumble in here looking for the Musical Box across the street. Once you're inside, though, the close quarters aid the socialization process. Retreat to the back room and play pool with blue-haired punks or an Anthony Michael Hall look-alike. The back room also houses the aforementioned jukebox, home to Weezer, Belle and Sebastian, the Who, My Bloody Valentine and other cult faves. Thank God Mona's still has a hold on the neighborhood, as countless French bistros and Italian trattorias have sprouted up on Avenue B.

Perks: pool, jukebox, video games, TVs

Dive factor: 6

Montero Bar and Grill

718-624-9799
73 Atlantic Avenue, at Hicks Street, Brooklyn Heights, Brooklyn
Subway Directions: 2/3/4/5 to Borough Hall, M/N/R to Court Street

My friend Beth, who craves a little dive bar adventure as much as yours truly, took the long, lonely walk down Atlantic Avenue with me one evening in search of this near-legendary bar. As our tired feet fortunately learned at the end of our journey, every step was worth it. Montero's is truly a slice of New York history, as things in this remote Brooklyn dive seem unchanged from decades past. Plenty of nostalgic photos and nautical-themed tchotchkes adorn the walls, undoubtedly a nod to the many longshoreman and sailors that have probably stumbled in here over the years (Montero's is located a few blocks from the docks). There are also cheap bottles of icy cold beer, crooners like Sinatra on the jukebox, and an inviting pool table in the back.

The salty crowd is like a family, a drunken, seafaring, dysfunctional family. They indulge the youngster taking his first step toward cirrhosis, or the old man who decides that it's a good idea at 3 a.m. to pull out the tambourine and shake along to the jukebox. If you could belong to the Montero family, trust me, you'd never go home again (you probably couldn't find home, and if you did, your relatives would never let you back in). Rumor has it that the gritty scenes from *Last Exit To Brooklyn* were filmed here; even if they weren't, they could have been. And that alone makes Montero's worth the trip.

Perks: pool, jukebox

Dive factor: 7

Best After-Work Dives

Desmond's
Rudy's
Jeremy's Ale House
Jimmy's Corner
Nancy Whiskey

Motor City

212-358-1595
127 Ludlow Street, between Rivington and Delancey Street
Subway Directions: F to Delancey Street, J/M/Z to Essex Street

The first time I ventured into Motor City, I was scared it might just be a New York theme-parky version of what a dive in burnt-out Detroit would look like. But to my relief I found that the place was filled with a hard-drinking, hard-living crowd. The bar is an homage to Detroit (duh!), and with its collection of cool backseats, steering wheels, car mirrors, a giant Ford sign, and other vintage paraphernalia, the only thing missing is Ted Nugent. All the hot-rod décor will make even a wimp feel manly.

The soundtrack is an inspired mix of punk and garage rock unless the DJ is feeling adventurous, and the music is blared at ear-splitting levels. Live bands also play once in a while—it's tight quarters when a band is in here. At one show, I witnessed a singer putting out a cigarette on his guitarist's arm; luckily the guitarist was a heroin addict who could handle his pain.

I should also note that anything goes here—whether its down-home fun like strawberry birthday cake being served to strangers, or my friend Beth setting her hair on fire (an accident, blame it on too many hair products and trying to light a cigarette). Thankfully, most tourists haven't discovered this little slice of Motor City down in the Lower East Side. And if you're way uptown (105th & Columbus), check out the rather punky but homey Ding Dong Lounge, from Motor City's former owners.

Perks: kick-ass DJs, videogames, occasional live music

Dive factor: 3

Best Dives To Take a Date

Botanica
Milady's
O'Connor's
Mare Chiaro

Nancy Whiskey Pub

212-226-9943
1 Lispenard Street, at West Broadway
Subway Directions: A/C/E to Canal Sreet

This log-cabinesque outpost would fit better in the rural mountains of upstate New York than on the border of Soho and Tribeca. The cool homey exterior, with a little thatched roof, sets it apart aesthetically from the rest of the neighborhood, as does the overwhelmingly male crowd, which is made up primarily of firemen, cops and postal workers (an increasingly insane mailman kept offering to sit with us while we were there, to "keep us company"). One pal of mine says he feels reassured drinking amongst civil servants—finally some government work we can all agree on.

Nancy Whiskey is also a home to the Irish—the name is taken from a traditional Irish folk song (check out Shane MacGowan's version). The regulars are content talking to one another, but if you ask nicely, they'll teach you how to play the shuffleboard game adjacent to the bar (it's harder than it looks).

In keeping with the rural mountain theme, there are plenty of wooden tables in the back, and in the quaint upstairs room. Note that, with the puzzling maze of streets down here, Nancy Whiskey can feel like a mountain outpost the first time you try to get there. But after you find it once, you shouldn't forget your way.

All in all, Nancy Whiskey is the perfect respite if you are in the mood for a hole-in-the-wall but stuck in this chichi neighborhood or in need of a drink at 9 a.m. One pal of mine has sour memories of Nancy Whiskey, though— he once met a blind date named Nancy here, only to find out she'd invited along eight other guys she'd also met online.

Perks: shuffleboard, jukebox , darts

Dive factor: 7

Nevada Smith's

212-982-2591
74 Third Avenue
Subway Directions: L to Third Ave., L/N/W/R/W/4/5/6 to Union Square
www.nevadasmiths.net

Some dive connoisseurs would argue that Nevada Smith's is more of a sports bar than a dive bar, but to me it's a sports dive bar (or a divey sports bar?), hence its inclusion in this book. Nevada Smith's is *the place* for the slumming sports enthusiast/nut, particularly for fans of European football (what we Americans call soccer). This place is a virtual shrine during World Cup time, and Nevada's is known as one of the most die-hard soccer bars in New York. If you want that feel of being in the stands during a game, pressed against your fellow fan to the point of asphyxiation, Nevada's is the place to be.

For the non-sports fan, Nevada's is a welcoming place to wile away a summer afternoon. One summer, back in my intern days, when I was living in the NYU dorm across the street, we used to retreat to Nevada Smith's during our frequent air conditioning outages. It's also an ideal spot for a pre- or post-movie drink—the Sony Village is next door. And, even on non-soccer nights, Nevada's has its share of interesting goings on: one 4th of July evening after fireworks on the FDR drive, my friends and I stumbled in here and found a man on stilts and another man with a large snake draped over his shoulders. $2 Bud, Bud Light, and Michelob Lights served from noon to midnight will have your inhibitions loosened as well.

The joint may be named for the 1966 film *Nevada Smith*, but chances are slim you'll spot Steve McQueen hanging out (since he died 20 years ago), although Sting and Simon Le Bon have stopped by to watch "footie."

Perks: 20 TVs, karaoke on Tuesday nights, soccer, soccer, soccer!

Dive factor: 3

Night Café

212-864-8889
938 Amsterdam Avenue, between 106th and 107th Street
Subway Directions: 1 to 110th Street, B/C to 110th Sreet

A confession: a few friends and I once took a bartending class at the "esteemed" Columbia School of Mixology. We passed with a straight A Absolut Average, but only because my pal Kristyn decided to smooch our 21-year-old "professor" the week before the final exam. The only place to go after class was the Night Café, a gem of a bar that attracts Columbia students and neighborhood drinkers, especially those into pool and darts. Add a good jukebox, plenty of beer, video games, board games, backgammon, and trivia night on Sundays, and you have a divey treat for the intellectual elite! And you'll only get smarter with each shot—with any shooter, you can get a bottle of Bud Light for only $1.

Keep in mind that the Columbia connection is heavy here—once another friend of mine met a Columbia student for what he thought was a date, but found his "date" accompanied by "four guys from her program." However, there is always enough of a local crowd present to allow you to avoid the Columbia gang and go blue collar.

Another confession: Kristyn wasn't alone in her Columbia transgression—after a few shots at the place to celebrate my MxA (Masters in Mixology), I found myself hooking up with a Columbia student several years my junior—thank god he was over 21.

Perks: trivia, pool, old board games, darts, jukebox, seemingly smart conversation with Columbia students, dart team and softball team

Dive factor: 4

Sporty Dives

Desmond's
Nevada Smith's
Jeremy's Ale House
Jimmy's Corner
Sandy's

O'Connor's

718-783-9721
39 Fifth Avenue, between Bergen and Dean Street, Park Slope, Brooklyn
Subway Directions: 2/3 to Bergen Street., Q/2/3/4/5 to Atlantic Avenue, M/N/R/W to Pacific Street

O'Connor's has officially made the leap from hard-drinking old-man bar (proudly serving since 1933) to hipster paradise—evident because even Manhattanites are making the trip to this saloon on the fringes of Park Slope. Now that the crowds are here, the place can become packed on weekends, but at off-times it still maintains a bit of its old man Brooklyn appeal.

It's not really the best place to fly solo unless you want to settle in and read the latest Jonathan Lethem book while nursing a bottled beer (no drafts here). Folks are friendly for the most part, but definitely not looking for action—they generally stick to themselves at the tables and booths. The old-timers who still cling to the few barstools can be chatty if you want them to—once when I met a date here, one of the regulars told me I smelled good (I *did* smell good, but my lame date never noticed). And if you're having one of THOSE days, note that O'Connor's opens at 8 a.m.

The jukebox is a big draw, mostly British Invasion gems plus more recent indie rock. There's no shortage of Elliott Smith tunes, and Mr. Smith himself used to scrawl lyrics on cocktail napkins when he lived in the area. Also enjoy the delightful collection of Margaret Keane artwork adorning the walls and the wacky old movie clips shown on the TVs. Conveniently, the bar is only about a block from another great local hangout, Freddy's, so by all means make it a two-bar run. Oh, and an update; if you didn't get along with a certain attitude-laden bartender here, you can come back, 'cause he's gone!

Perks: occasional bands, great jukebox

Dive factor: 7

O' Connor's

O'Hanlon's

212-473-9384
349 E. 14th Street, between 1st and 2nd Avenue
Subway Directions: L to First Avenue

At press time, I'm sad to report that O'Hanlon's is undergoing a face-lift that will turn its rough-around-the-edges facade into a standard-looking pub. I'm hoping that the inside of the bar retains its working-class character as an Irish bar with a key location (right by the L train on 14th and First) and a bit of subversive flair.

The crowd is mostly male, firemen and construction worker types, with the occasional oddball such as a bodybuilder with a permed ponytail, and a Wall Streeter who bored my friends and I one night with tales of his old chimney sweeping business. Drinks aren't terribly cheap—pints are mostly over $4—but you get served by a real Irish bartender who knows how to draw a real Guinness.

O'Hanlon's doesn't offer any moments for quiet contemplation, as the jukebox is always turned up to 11. The jukebox selections don't seem that important, since the guys lined up at the bar have their eyes peeled to the six different TV sets. Journey and Yes seem to be jukebox faves, but you can sometimes hear surprises like AC/DC's "Back in Black" or a track from the *Xanadu* soundtrack.

Serious dart lovers will feel at home here, as O'Hanlon's was voted NYC's best darts bar.

Perks: TVs, jukebox, darts

Dive factor: 3

Best Outdoor Drinking

Reif's Tavern
Jeremy's Ale House
Between the Bridges
Alibi
Bohemian Hall

Old Homestead

212-420-9668
102 First Avenue, between 6th and 7th Street
Subway Directions: 6 to Astor Place, F/V to Second Avenue

The Old Homestead is one of those places that you've probably walked past a hundred times but never ventured into, or even noticed. But you're in for a good, cheap Eastern European time if you step past the unassuming facade (there's no neon sign, only the fading bar name painted discreetly above the door). The place does feel like a local neighborhood hangout, but only if you're local neighborhood is a Krakow suburb. Weekdays the crowd is comprised mostly of Eastern European blue-collar guys chatting in their native tongues and swilling big bottles of Okocim, a tasty (and strong) Polish brew. Weekends the place gets a bit rowdier, as the TV set playing "Wheel of Fortune" is replaced by jukebox tunes (an eclectic mix that combines plenty of polka with the Spice Girls, Steve Miller Band, Mariah Carey, loads of Beatles and, surprisingly, one Talking Heads disc).

The décor (using that word is a stretch) has a very no-frills '70s vibe thanks to lots of fake wood and old wallpaper in hues of brown and orange. Christmas tinsel up year round is one of the few festive touches, along with some tchotchkes, such as ceramic cat figurines behind the bar and a photo collage of regulars near the pool table. It's not dirty per se, but the place has been around for 15 or so years and looks its age. One regular I encountered, who told me he had stopped into the Old Homestead nearly every day for five years admitted that the place "should be cleaned up."

My friend Matt told me that once he got into a brawl at the pool table with two "very large, unfriendly Germans" who broke a pool cue on his friend's back, so beware. Definitely not to be confused with the steakhouse of the same name—there's no filet mignon here.

Perks: pool, jukebox, video game, TV, Okocim

Dive Factor: 7

NOTE: Sadly, the Old Homestead has closed it's doors permanently since the guide's first printing. It is gone, but not forgotten, and we will miss it.

119 Bar

212-777-6158
119 E. 15th Street, between Irving Plaza and Union Square East
Subway Directions: L/N/Q/R/W/4/5/6 to Union Square

One of my worst barhopping nights in New York happened around Union Square. I was out with my roommate, our mutual friend from Chicago, and two pretentious assholes that were invited by said mutual friend. I had to suffer through namedropping at the Belmont Lounge, money flashing at the Lemon, and model watching at the Union Bar. After that night, I vowed never to return to the Union Square area for any kind of alcoholic-related social festivity.

Thank God I have since been introduced to 119, Union Square's donation to the dive realm (inhabiting a space that once contained a Polish veterans' social club). This is the prefect spot to grab a pre-band drink before heading to nearby venue Irving Plaza. Of course everyone else realizes that too, so it's insanely crowded pre- and post-show. The crowd is made up of NYU kids, area artists and thespians, and would-be indie rock stars—think guys who dress like they belong in the Strokes and the girls who love them because they can't date a guy who's really in the Strokes.

The 119 has an interesting layout—you enter through the spacious "pool room" and then walk through into a dimly lit, rather sultry main room where the bar is located. There is also a side room that offers private seating spaces, which looks to be a great make-out spot, although I've yet to personally test this hypothesis.

As you'd expect from the rock-and-roll vibe, the jukebox has a great alt-rock mix. You may even be tempted to skip the show and stay put at the 119 instead.

Perks: jukebox, pool, darts, DJs on Friday and Saturdays spinning old rock and '80s punk

Dive factor: 5

169 BAR

169 Bar

212-473-8866
169 E. Broadway, between Rutgers Street and Jefferson Street
Subway Directions: F to East Broadway

This bar's cool retro sign always attracted my attention when I visited my pal David in his co-op high-rise across the street, so I was eager to check out this outpost near Chinatown. Imagine my disappointment when I made it inside, and to my horror saw the trappings of a near-lounge. The place was aflame with red candles, with brand new booths lining the outer walls, and a DJ booth in the back. A menu on the table listed $45 champagne and calamari! *Quelle horreur*, this was not the dive I was expecting! However, the 169 Bar soon taught me a valuable lesson in not judging a bar by its velvet cover. On closer inspection, I saw Coors Light next to the champagne on the menu. Then I saw Ms. Pac-Man and a weird filthy old fish tank by the DJ booths. Things were looking up, or should I say down?

An old dirty fan stood in the corner, covered with the grime that was missing from the red candleholders. The jukebox started belting out some bad Allman Brothers tunes, followed by some George Thorogood and then Meatloaf's "Paradise By the Dashboard Light." A strange woman came and sat, uninvited, at our table to tell us about the free chess lessons at the library across the street. I sensed we were inching closer and closer to dive status, when, lo and behold, a brawl broke out over a pool game in the back. Ding, ding, ding—we have a winner! Bloodshed, swearing in two languages (English and Español), and a broken pool cue—it doesn't get much divier than that. To top it off, the "Macarena" was playing in the background as the blows were dealt (I couldn't make this up if I tried). Immediately following the fight, a crusty neighborhood woman sitting at the bar—slamming a white Russian, no less—yelled at some guy to "go fuck himself," while two other old men mumbled to themselves. Thank god the generic lounge-esque trappings didn't stop this place from having a little spark to it. To the bar's credit, a guy from the kitchen came out to make sure we knew that fighting wasn't a common occurrence.

Perks: food, pool, jukebox, DJ nights, TVs, occasional brawls

Dive Factor: 4

P & G Café

P&G Café

212-874-8568
279 Amsterdam Avenue, at 73rd Street
Subway Directions: 1/2/3 to 72nd Street

My friend Spesh has dubbed this place "Jack Wagner's" because she and her pal Matt once saw Mr. Wagner in here playing air guitar to AC/DC's "Back in Black." Matt noted that this was around the time that Sebastian Bach had replaced the aging soap star in Broadway's *Jekyll & Hyde*, so maybe Jack was drowning his sorrows. If that was the case, then Jack picked the perfect place to come for a little anonymous self-pitying. P & G is an unassuming bar where locals stop in for a few, starting at 10 a.m., and nobody pays much attention to what anybody else is doing.

Though some of the old-timers look as if they've been coming in since the bar opened in 1941 (and they don't seem too eager to make new friends), the crowd on the whole feels a bit collegiate, probably because most people hunker down in the booths college-style to enjoy reasonably priced pitchers and a decent menu of bar food. Don't come in here planning on mingling; it's the kind of place where you come with a small group to shoot the shit or commiserate by yourself over your lost Broadway role.

The interior has such a classic bar look that it has been filmed as a New York watering hole in *Donnie Brasco*, *Runaway Bride*, and *Seinfeld*. There's also a great old neon sign out front. I can't promise that Jack Wagner will ever reappear, but the Allman Brothers are known to stop in when they play their annual gigs at the Beacon Theater a few blocks away. And my friend Pookie recently spotted the entire cast of *Oz* in here.

Perks: food, pitchers, jukebox, Ms. Pac-Man, celebrity sightings

Dive factor: 4

Parkside Lounge

Parkside Lounge

212-673-6270
317 E. Houston St, between Avenues B and C
Subway Directions: F/V to Second Avenue
www.parksidelounge.com

Don't worry, The Parkside is not a real "lounge"—it's a great old dive that's been here more than 50 years, long before the letters "LES" stood for a cool, hipper-than-thou neighborhood that shall remain nameless. The cool old neon sign out front is brighter than anything inside—expect gross carpeting and a bit of a stale smell from 50 years old of accumulated smoke, beer, vomit, and other bodily excretions better left to the imagination. Aside from heavy drinking, especially during happy hour, there are other diversions like pinball, pool, and a solid jukebox.

Because of its huge bar area, the Parkside is a great place to convene a group for warming up, wasting away an evening, or winding down (lots of wait staffers like to come in here after the restaurants close). The slightly out of the way location allows it to avoid the Bridge and Tunnelers that crowd the other area dives, particularly on weekends. In addition, there is a back room that plays host to local indie bands, comedy nights, salsa dancing, and occasional readings (though I wouldn't count on a heavy literary quotient—a friend of mine tried to stage a reading here, and was blown off by the supposedly interested owner.)

If, by chance, you find that the place isn't cool enough for you, consider this—my friend Dave spotted his idol Björk in here one night while grooving to a Latin band.

Perks: backroom for music and assorted theme nights (comedy, readings), jukebox, pool

Dive factor: 7

Worst Bathrooms

Mars
Village Idiot
Sweetwater
Mare Chiaro (men's room)
Smith's

Phil Hughes

212-722-9415
1682 First Avenue, at 87th Street
Subway Directions: 6 to 86th Street

During my first foray to the Phil Hughes, my friends and I were the only people in here under 60. Lining up while most of the world is heading off to work, solo old men sit at the bar with their morning papers, and will still be sitting there at the end of the day. Nothing seems to faze these old-timers, whether its pairs of young folks heading to the bathroom to make out, or the guy running a business for his "sweet ladies" from his cell phone. Just don't try to engage anyone in too much conversation, and for God's sake, don't make the mistake I did of playing ABBA on the jukebox. Let's just say Sweden's greatest export wasn't a real crowd-pleaser—the traditional Irish tunes on the jukebox go over much better.

This is a scary place where old men rule, but if you really need a dive bar on the Upper East Side, it's the real deal. I discovered Phil Hughes (otherwise known as Phil Collins to my pals) through a certain pal of mine who meets her man here fairly regularly. If you're jonesing for your stuff at 8 a.m. after a long night out, trekking up to the Phil Hughes can make you feel all right!

There are two special perks associated with Phil Collins, I mean Hughes. First, the place isn't crowded—there's usually a seat at the long bar or at the tables that fill the rest of the room. Second, it is quite possibly the only bar on the Upper East Side not frequented by frat boys.

Perks: jukebox

Dive factor: 9

Phoenix

212-477-9979
447 E. 13th Street, between 1st Avenue and Avenue A
Subway Directions: L to First Avenue

This relative newcomer to the East Village gay scene has the relaxed feel of your hometown pub, if you happen to come from Provincetown. A long, old wooden bar, and a welcoming attitude to both men and canines (and ladies, for that matter), make one and all feel like they fit right in. In addition, the Phoenix sports one of the best jukeboxes —gay or straight—in town, full of R.E.M., Outkast, Lambchop, T. Rex, Belle & Sebastian, Fugazi, Nancy Sinatra and the *Repo Man* soundtrack. (I would become a gay man just to become a regular here so I could listen to the jukebox over and over again.)

The bar includes the usual amenities—a pool table, pinball machines, Ms. Pac-Man—plus some nice touches, such as paintings of flames on the airshafts. The side room is cozy with church pews and pornographic pictures on the tables, but my friends who visit the Phoenix frequently assure me the main room is where the action is. (One pal confides: "The side room is like death. Nobody goes in there.") Except for dollar beer nights on Mondays, drinks aren't cheap—I paid $16.50 for three *almost* moderately-sized mixed drinks—but if you want to feel like you are getting a bargain, remember that drinks are less expensive here than at the Cock, which is around the corner.

After a few visits, you'll start to see the same familiar faces. It isn't a very cruisey scene, but you can probably score if you really want to. Wednesday is dollar night, and the bartenders are friendly and easy with the buybacks. (Once, my friend Gary walked to the bar for his first round and was told, "Honey, you've been buying all night. These are on me.") The pool table has one great rule, which should be a law at all bars: "Remember, it's just a game so don't act like a dumb ass."

Perks: jukebox, video games, pool

Dive factor: 3

Raccoon Lodge

212-766-9656
59 Warren Street, at West Broadway
Subway Directions: 1/2/A/C to Chambers Street

212-874-9984
480 Amsterdam Avenue, at 83rd Street
Subway Directions: 1/2 to 86th Street

212-650-1775
1439 York Avenue, between 76th-77th Street
Subway Directions: 6 to 77th Street

The Raccoon Lodge, with three branches in Manhattan, gets its name from the Ralph Kramden boys club in *The Honeymooners*. The York Avenue branch is a great respite from the fratboy hangouts on the Upper East Side. In early evening, you'll find a real mix of characters—old men drinking martinis alongside mustachioed blue-collar types enjoying $2 drafts of Rolling Rock, along with the stray indefinable divestar. The night I was there it was a dude wearing a "Who the Fuck is Eddie Van Halen?" T-shirt, the shirt my friend David once wore to one of my White Trash parties.

The interior is fairly generic, but refreshingly spacious, and the bathrooms are amazingly clean (ladies, enjoy that full-length mirror, a rarity in dive bars). Saturday nights bring a karaoke crowd, which had me running for the exits before anyone was drunk enough to attempt to sing "The Lady in Red," or something in a similar vein. The bartenders were personable without having any real personality, but the bouncer was a friendly sort who noticed one of my friends was wearing a Dungeon T-shirt (a bar in New Orleans), and struck up a conversation about his time in the Crescent City.

Though you wouldn't bat an eye at the joint if it were in the East Village, on the Upper East Side it's a must-stop. $8 pitchers of Rolling Rock all day are another reason to settle in. The legendary downtown branch is an ideal place to find Wall Streeters who want to let their close-cropped hair down.

Perks: pool, TVs, ATM machine, Ms. Pac-Man, video golf, jukebox

Dive factor: 4

Red Rock West Saloon

212-366-5359
457 W. 17th Street, at Tenth Avenue
Subway Directions: A/C/E to 14th Sreet., L to 8th Avenue

I stumbled onto Red Rock West, or "the Rock" if you will, after a night of too many open-bar, schmoozy-film-and-music-biz parties. At our last stop before the Rock (nearby chichi bar The Park), what looked like 19-year-old models were sandwiched on the patio, drinking $8 Heinekens. There were thankfully no models at The Rock, and no $8 beers either. What I found was a spacious, full old bar with a few tourists (more evidently come here on weekends), some union workers, and die-hard drinkers from the area's docks. The de rigueur outfit for ladies was jeans and black tank tops, but nobody minded that I was overdressed, or that a woman in white lace shirt, bleached jeans, and heels was a walking fashion victim.

The décor is pure dive, from the hand-lettered bathroom signs, to the skull in a noose behind the bar, the Made in the USA license plate, and the bumper sticker that reads "Don't drink and drive, you might hit a bump and spill your beer." A bonus is bartenders that actually seem to enjoy their jobs. The one I spoke to, Jessica, was refreshingly real, and seemed to be into it for something more than just the tips. She got some New Orleans tourists to dance on the bar (none too well), held an impromptu Billy Idol sneer contest, and made me and my new pals some mighty tasty shots with apple schnapps. It was like being at Hogs and Heifers or the Village Idiot, without the obviously forced and scripted routines.

The barkeeps don't take any shit—a sign behind the bar says "look all you want but keep your hands off." They shout through their loudspeaker that they'll skip "shitty music" if you play the wrong song on the jukebox (Madonna, the Cars). And you'd better play nice—the bouncers are *huge.*

It's hard to have a bad time here; if you find yourself bored, just talk to the regulars. I did, and ended up smooching a gentleman with tattooed testicles (all in the name of research of course).

Perks: pool, jukebox

Dive factor: 7

Reif's Tavern

212-426-0519
302 E. 92nd Street, between 1st and 2nd Avenues
Subway Directions: 6 to 95th Street
www.reifstavern.com

My friend Pookie, who lives a few blocks from Reif's, and I had been meaning to check out this place out for ages—it looks like a place with real character stuck amidst the cookie-cutter brownstones of the Upper East Side (yes, brownstones can be boring). When we finally ventured in one Saturday night with a group of five pals, we were not disappointed. Reif's is like three bars in one—the front is the sort of no-frills bar that attracts neighborhood old-timers, the middle room feels like a rec room circa 1982, and finally, there is a nice patio out back to complete the trifecta.

Friendly owner Eddie (aka "Hank") treats everyone like a potential regular, but judging from all the Yankees memorabilia, Mets fans might want to steer clear, or at least keep their mouths shut. The neighborhood crowd is friendly, too, ready to offer my pal Brooke some chicken salad from their BBQ without a second thought. I dug the classic rock tunes featuring the likes of Pat Benatar and REO Speedwagon. And if things start getting dull, just stand back and ask Eddie to perform his fire-breathing trick.

The 11 a.m. opening time means that the patio can provide a prime day-drinking and eating spot. Though you're unlikely to pass by this out-of-the way joint—it's on a residential block where the biggest attraction seems to be a car wash—Reif's warrants an exploratory trip. Although my friend Sara visited and says the one word to sum up the place was "sticky." If you want some insurance that it's your type of place before trekking here, check out their website, where you can read about and view photos of the barkeeps and patrons.

Perks: darts, pool, jukebox, outdoor patio

Dive factor: 6 (front bar), 1 (patio)

Ruby's Bar & Grill

No Phone
Boardwalk and Stillwell Avenue, Coney Island, Brooklyn
Subway Directions: F/Q/W to Coney Island-Stillwell Avenue

It's a good thing that the fluorescent lights at Ruby's are way, way too bright—otherwise I might have been tempted to move to Coney Island and become a regular (next thing you know, I'd be reliving *Requiem for a Dream* by stealing TVs and whoring myself for drugs). This Coney Island landmark, 80 years old and owned by the same family for the last 65 years (as one of the family members behind the bar proudly told me), has a prime spot on the boardwalk near famed attractions like Nathan's hot dog stand and the Cyclone roller coaster. It proudly wears its Coney heritage, displaying hundreds of fascinating old Coney Island photographs along the walls—in yellowing frames, you can see Coney Island in its heydey. The long, narrow bar adjoins a grill area where you can try your luck with fresh oysters or any variety of heavily fried food (I opted for a corn dog, my first in probably two decades). Even sitting at a stool in the back of the bar, you have a great view of the blue Atlantic, and if you want a closer beach feel, you can grab one of the plastic tables outside. How beautifully idyllic it all sounds, right?

However, what is not so beautifully idyllic is the crowd. By the light of the aforementioned silvery fluorescent bulb, I was able to come face to face with the faces of Ruby's. And what a bunch of faces they were: an 80-year-old Hispanic man in a sailor's hat; a man wearing a fancy silk vest with no shirt underneath; a guy with a tattoo of a red lipstick trace on his neck; an elderly man muttering and dancing to himself by the jukebox; and a tourist wearing a "Whoop Ass Machine" T-shirt. Yes, the official freak shows of Coney Island may be long gone, but you can still find plenty of unofficial freaks at Ruby's.

The drinks are fairly cheap: $3 bottles of beer, poured into a cup for you whether you like it or not, or a $5 premium mixed drink that's small but strong. If wine's your poison, don't expect an on-call vintner here; just pick one of the tiny twist-off bottles displayed behind the bar. Aesthetically, if sitting at the bar and staring at empty beer boxes, stacks of duct tape and a broken stereo isn't your scene, gather at one of the old Formica tables, or at the strange grouping of a sectional couch and a marble-topped coffee table (a hand-me-down from Grandpa Ruby perhaps?).

The most pleasant surprise is the jukebox, which offers something for everyone: Jimmy Roselli, Rosemary Clooney, Johnny Maestro and the Brooklyn Bridge for the old neighborhood folks; Def Leppard, Poison, and Milli Vanilla for '80s enthusiasts; Kenny Rogers, Reba McIntire, and Billy Ray Cyrus for the country set. And Bob Marley because it just seems appropriate for the beach. The crowd seemed to dig my segue from "Crimson and Clover" into Journey's "Separate Ways."

Amenities: food, jukebox, sells T-shirts

Dive factor: 7

Rudy's

Rudy's

212-974-9169
627 Ninth Avenue, between 44th and 45th Street
Subway Directions: A/C/E to 42nd Street/Port Authority

Three words sum up the Rudy's experience: Free Hot Dogs. Plus mustard if you so desire. Where else in Manhattan can you find such a deal? And as my friend Brian has demonstrated to me time and again, there is no one-dog limit, so eat to your cholesterol's content!

Though Rudy's borders the theater district, you'll find more Hell's Kitchen neighbors than tourists in this joint. (Maybe they're tipped off by the giant pig statue propped outside.) The crowd is usually pretty tipsy (less pitchers, more hot dogs!) and can get kind of cruisey at times, but not in an obnoxious way. Unless you encounter some folks still here from the 8 a.m. $4 Miller Lite pitcher special, the clientele consists primarily of blue collar types, office workers, an a few artsy folks sprinkled in. And everybody seems to get along well. Hell, some people even go out of their way to be friendly—once I was with some galpals (who were, yes, attractive), and a stranger apparently overheard us complaining of hunger, and next thing we knew, we had a bag full of junk food from the bodega down the street. Every time I turn around, someone else has a new Rudy's story for me, none better than the tale of the crazy old women who professed her love for a bunch of gay men and then offered them a wad of old sushi from her purse (!). Hang around long enough and you can play brain teasers with visiting foreign pilots (one even emailed me an answer to a toughie the next week) or you can find locals who'll take you to nearby underground casinos.

In addition to the hot dogs, Rudy's also wins favor thanks to the plentiful pitchers of beer (somewhat of a rarity in NYC) and the classy selections of jazz greats on the jukebox. It feels like part of the old neighborhood—Rudy's has been here since 1934. The place a bit run-down inside, but that doesn't stop throngs of people from packing the joint nightly. If you're lucky, you'll score one of the duct-tape-covered booths; otherwise you'll be stuck at the crowded bar. In the summer, there are some seats available in a "garden" area—it's like an abandoned parking lot with booths that have had the tabletops ripped off.

Darkest Dives

Dick's
Bellvue
Library
Mars
Milano
Subway Inn
Sweetwater Tavern

The Sand Bar

718-474-4842
116th and Boardwalk, Rockaway Park, Queens
Subway Directions: A to Rockaway Park-Beach 116 Street (during off hours, take S from Broad Channel)

Before visiting the Sand Bar, my last visit to a beachfront bar had been the swank Delano Hotel in Miami's South Beach. Talk about a study in contrasts! Once I overcame the initial shock of the trashiness of Rockaway, I found this bar to be quite welcoming. (Maybe it reminds me of the Myrtle Beach jaunts of my high school days?) Plus, I saw the finest mullet I've ever seen in NYC here.

After dealing with the crowds on the beach—think ghettoblasters pumping Hot 97, hairy men in Speedos, and 14-year-old girls strutting in bikinis and smoking cigarettes (oh the humanity!)—you're going to need a beer, and the Sand Bar can certainly deliver, if only during summer. The food counter on one side of the room offers pizza, fried chicken, fish & chips, hot dogs and the like. The other side of the room is a simple rectangular bar with stools on all sides, where they sell canned beer. (Note: evidently some folks need to use straws to drink beer out of a can.) There are a few tables out front in the sun by the boardwalk. Beware the biting flies!

As you might expect from a beach bar, most of the men are shirtless, proud of their potbellies and tattoos (not cool tribal designs, but instead eagles, flags, or "mom"). There are definitely a few characters in this group of leathery gents—a guy with flip-up sunglasses, a 70-year-old man with a sailor hat on. The music is half beachy (Beach Boys, Jan & Dean), half trashy (John Mellencamp, Mariah), which suits the place perfectly.

If this place is somehow too hip for you (doubtful!), there are two hard-drinking old-man bars on 116th Street: Rogers Irish House and PJ Curran. As you walk the few blocks back to the A train, you might want to check them out. (Or you might just want to run back to the train!)

Perks: TVs, jukebox, outdoor seating, ocean view, food

Dive factor: 8

Sandy's

212-599-9349
699 Second Avenue, between 37th and 38th Street
Subway Directions: 6 to 33rd Street

A good rule of thumb: the closer a bar is to a tunnel, the better the chance that it will be a dive. Sandy's, on the East Side near the Queens-Midtown tunnel, proves this hypothesis. My friend Melissa recommended the place, but with one warning: that the place is way too bright. And it is—but perhaps that's because the place is kinda sporty, with a big screen TV, world cup poster, pool table, and hockey decorations (Rangers jerseys and a hockey stick hang behind the bar). Sandy's is also a place for the serious dart enthusiast, as not only do they have a dart area (amateurs stay away!), they even sell dart accessories. A pinball machine called Sharkey's Shootout completes the bar's sports-related diversions.

Otherwise, the place is a bit Long Island-y. There were some preppies up front, some older guys in the back, and a regular who was dying to get my friends Chris and Sara to play backgammon with her. But we were content to sit and drink at the long bar, enjoy the classic rock on the jukebox (friendly regulars may load the juke and let you pick songs), and speculate as to why there was Bath & Body Works antibacterial lotion behind the bar. After about five or so drinks, Chris and Sara finally scored a buyback, but they said it was probably only because the bartender looked annoyed at the prospect of taking their money and making change.

Happy hour 'til 7 p.m. will get you $2 pints of Bud or Bud Light and $2 well drinks, or $3 pints of Sam Adams. If the Cheetos/Chex Mix-esque bar snacks don't soak up your beer, a pizza joint a few doors down serves the sort of plasticy cheese pizza that's perfect after a night of drinking.

Perks: pool, darts, jukebox, pinball

Dive factor: 6

Siberia

212-333-4141
356 W. 40th Street, at Ninth Avenue
Subway Directions: A/C/E to 42nd Street-Port Authority

Siberia holds a special place in my heart—and my beginnings with this legendary bar have a somewhat legendary quality all their own. I had heard mysterious tales of a unique bar buried in a Manhattan subway station with a great jukebox, and one night in 1998 after a few (okay, a dozen) drinks in midtown, my friend Melissa and I set off in search of the famed Siberia. We found it pretty easily, walked in the door, and were immediately greeted by a gregarious guy who asked us what we were drinking. Soon, we had two ice-cold beers in hand, and this man started to tell a joke—"What does a girl from West Virginia say after sex?" Before he could finish, I offered the punch line —"Get off me daddy, you're crushing my cigarettes!" And this beer-offering, joke-telling guy could tell he had some new friends. He turned out to be Tracy Westmoreland, the owner of Siberia, the first person I would call if I ever need to get bailed out of jail.

Siberia soon became one of my homes away from home. I was working two blocks away at the time, so another heavy-drinking editor, Michelle, and I would hit the place right after work, grab two stools at the miniscule bar, chat with our favorite bartender Dave and inevitably still be there making new friends at 1 a.m. Because it was like a dark little cave (below ground, in a subway corridor), it was easy to lose track of time in Siberia. Of course, it wasn't the location that kept us coming back, and it certainly wasn't the restrooms – some of the most disgusting I've ever encountered, but the clientele: a mix of hard-drinking gossip columnists, MTV producers, strippers, and other assorted citizens. The kick-ass jukebox only added to the ambiance. Siberia became the scene of many events in my life – birthdays, infamous "white trash" parties, and assorted adventurous evenings being propositioned against the pinball machine.

But the dream couldn't live forever. In 2000, Siberia lost its lease (blame the evil bastards at the Rockefeller Group). Tracy even went so far as to travel to Japan, the home of Mitsubishi, the parent of the Rockefeller Group, to protest, chaining himself to a toilet in the process. But he couldn't save the space. So that version of Siberia is now just a fond memory (and a documentary film). But Siberia still lives—adjacent to Tracy's other bar,

Bellevue, in Hell's Kitchen. The new space is much bigger and airier, and not quite as smoky, scary or covered in graffiti. Yet it still has more character than most spaces in Manhattan. Most of the bartenders from the old joint are gone, but the new ones will treat you like family, provided you're not cursing, obnoxiously hitting on women, or generally acting like a "meathead"—if so, Tracy will have you out on the street—I'm serious. Oldtimers such as myself may mourn the old space, but the new one still retains some of the flavor—you can find films, comedy, music (or just hanging) in the downstairs room, and an unusual mix of folks at the upstairs bar. You may even catch a glimpse of Russell Crowe, the *SNL* cast, or Anthony Bourdain (the *Kitchen Confidential* author who hangs here frequently), or perhaps a glimpse of gay porn being projected onto the walls (to scare off the frat boys).

But, dammit, I still miss the rattle of the subway cars and the old tarp-covered couch at the old building. Thank god they salvaged one of the toilets (hanging like a trophy above the new bar). Look for the red light and be prepared for some adventure.

Perks: pinball, jukebox, live entertainment, photo booth

Dive factor: 7

Best Bathrooms

Raccoon Lodge
Barrow's Pub
Leisure Time Bowling Center
Motor City
Rudy's

Sidestreet Saloon

718-448-6868
11 Schuyler Street, Staten Island
Travel Directions: Walk from the Staten Island Ferry Terminal

My friend Jason, who lives nearby, assured me that the Sidestreet was "a true dive, and the few neighborhood hipsters that do go there don't go because they think it's cool." After my visit, I concur that it's not that cool. On first glance, it didn't seem that divey either, but the crowd soon changed my mind. There was the old gentleman next to me who was wearing earplugs for the first hour or so he was there, just so he didn't have to talk to people. He had a transistor radio with him, an old army jacket on despite the 90-degree heat, and two cocktail umbrellas stuck in his hat. Most remarkably, he was haggling with the pretty young bartender over 25 cents—he thought his Bud drafts should cost $2.75, not $3. Next to him was a non-regular, a good-looking professional guy toting a backgammon board, with a completely glazed look in his eye. He paid for his one drink with a $50 bill and then asked, rather confusedly, for a taxi. My friend Michelle and I guessed he may have been coming off a coke bender.

Overall, the place isn't that strange, just a good neighborhood bar if your neighborhood happens to be two blocks from the Staten Island Ferry terminal. There is a jukebox with Pat Benatar and Motown hits, a full menu of food (the burgers would be a safer bet than the mussels), TVs playing NY1, and a lotto machine with a funny "liquor before lotto" sign nearby.

Occasional live music and karaoke pack in the locals, and be prepared for a crowd anytime there's a game at the nearby ballpark where the Staten Island Yankees play. The crowd from the courthouse next door also wanders in for lunch or a few brews.

The Sidestreet has been here for about 13 years, replacing what the bartender dubbed a "classy restaurant" called Montezuma. While I wouldn't look for fine dining this close to the ferry terminal, I would definitely recommend the Sidestreet for a few beers or a bite to eat.

Perks: food, jukebox, TVs, lotto, karaoke, bands

Dive factor: 4

Smith's

212-246-3268
701 Eighth Avenue, at 44th Street
Subway Directions: A/C/E to 42nd Street-Port Authority

If there's one thing I hate about a dive bar, it's too much light. Do we REALLY need to see our grimy surroundings and less-savory fellow patrons in such glorious detail? Unfortunately, there are no shadowy recesses for canoodling in Smith's, but this brightly-lit spot does offer other amenities, namely plenty of food served at the spacious back booths behind the bar. Beer isn't cheap, $4.50 a pint for some brands, but the diverse draft selection was a definite bonus.

The long bar and nondescript space give Smith's the feel of a hotel bar (think Howard Johnson's in Dubuque, not the Standard in LA). The crowd included some genial Irishmen, a few tourists who probably were looking for somewhere a bit nicer, a handful of stragglers from Port Authority carrying their Duane Reade bags and a group of pink-cheeked youngsters enjoying some cheeseburger deluxes and a few pitchers. As is the norm for this area around Port Authority, at least one guy with a limp staggered into the place on an hourly basis.

The Irish bartender was incredibly welcoming, even if the crowd mostly kept to themselves. The regulars just sort of grunted to one another, but after a few hours of drinking, you could be their next buddy. That is, if you can stomach the stench coming out of the men's room and the musical accompaniment of Was Not Was' "Walk the Dinosaur." Good luck.

Perks: food served

Dive Factor: 6

Sneakers

212-242-9830
392 West Street, at Christopher Street
Subway Directions: 1/2 to Christopher St.-Sheridan Square
www.sneakers-nyc.com

Although Sneakers is located near both Chelsea (home of buff boys) and the West Village (home of pretty boys), the clientele here is a bit rougher around the edges (think lost boys). As the bar's website announces, the place boasts "a mix of men, all ages, colors, shapes and sizes feeling footloose and frisky." On a Friday night when we visited, not everybody was so footloose—one chap was nodding off in a corner despite the earsplitting Donna Summer tunes. The crowd was indeed astonishingly mixed—there was a Sammy Davis, Jr. look-alike, some British tourists at the pool table, a guy wearing sweatpants, a guy wearing all leather, and a classy businessman who brought in his underage boytoy who, for the record, clearly wasn't 21, and was asked to leave without being served! In true neighborhood bar fashion, most of the crowd seemed friendly and ready to welcome newcomers.

While the bar is near the Hudson River, the view is not as scenic as one might hope, unfortunately consisting of a bus stop out front and the traffic stuck on the West Side Highway, both seen through grimy, gate-covered windows. The interior décor is strictly dive bar 101—old Christmas lights, Mardi Gras beads, plus some personal touches like red duct tape covering the bar, a nude male pinup behind the cash register and the letters S & M painted on the bathroom doors. Mixed drinks were surprisingly pricey, but you can probably score a buyback. Plus, the free goldfish crackers on the bar went down surprisingly well with my can of Coors Light.

Perks: pool, free crackers at bar

Dive factor: 8

Sophie's

212-228-5680
507 E. 5th St. (Aves. A-B)
Subway Directions: F, V to Second Avenue., 6 to Astor Place, L to First Avenue

What you find at Sophie's all depends on when you go: one Thursday night about 7:30 (a reasonable hour to start drinking, mind you), I walked into dead silence, with only four patrons at the bar watching *The Simpsons*, possibly drooling. They didn't seem to want to be disturbed, although the cute indie boy bartender was courteous and two other visitors were soon racking up a game of pool and eating Cracker Jacks. However, one Saturday evening, the place was so packed that there was no room to stand. Smoke filled the air as boisterous groups gathered at the tables and a young college student sketched the motley scene with his charcoals.

Sophie's doesn't go out of its way to attract newcomers, hence no sign out front, but it does offer a welcoming vibe whether you're a newbie or a regular. It would seem like more of a Tom Waits kind of bar, but the jukebox is actually quite varied (European techno, Marvin Gaye, Sinead O'Connor, and some *Dawson's Creek* dreck). The clientele is just as diverse: one evening we saw an off-duty nurse, a scary man perusing a military magazine at the bar, a few neighborhood couples on dates, and a guy sporting a business suit and a mohawk. If you're too scared to approach the regulars, then you can befriend one of the dogs that is sure to be roaming the place.

The best spot in the house is the booth by the front window near a poor, poor plant that has bravely fought through years of smoke trying to breathe. In the back, things are usually a tight squeeze, with patrons jostling for the pool table or video games. The back also holds the bathroom, where I once tried to make out with a date. Such intimacy is not recommended—the place was too crowded and the long bathroom line got very angry!

Perks: pool, jukebox, video games

Dive factor: 7

Spinning Wheel

718-728-9716
25-06 Broadway, at 29th Street, Astoria, Queens
Subway Directions: N/W to Broadway

The first story I heard about the Wheel was from my friend Robert, who used to live nearby. He saw a man being literally thrown out of the bar, followed by a scream: "Don't ever come back, you fucking child molester."

The next time I heard of the Spinning Wheel was from my friend Matt, who still lives nearby. I was polling him about dives in his 'hood, and he told me "I really, really wouldn't recommend them. Be careful." This coming from someone who's seen me drinking in dives 'til dawn.

So I should have known what to be prepared for, but the Wheel still scared the hell out of me. I made the mistake of going alone, hoping to enjoy a few solitary drinks and do some reading. I got a frosty mug of Bud for only $1.75 and took a seat near the bar. Soon, a crazy old man came up to me saying I "looked and smelled beautiful," which was highly unlikely since I hadn't bathed or brushed my hair that day. He said he'd buy me a drink, but forgot about me and only begged the sassy bartender for "one more" for himself. She told him he'd been cut off. He begged, "one more for the road." She said, "The road is closed." He then started a 10-minute screaming match. A toothless 70-year-old woman to my right, who was drinking Bud ponys and chain-smoking Marlboros (two packs so far), yelled at him to get out. The rest of the drunks, mostly older men, shook their heads but didn't seem surprised. They stayed glued to the Mets game or the TVs broadcasting horse races from Belmont. After one more desperate plea for a drink (pledging his enduring love to the barkeep), the old guy was thrown out, and he headed to the OTB parlor next door. Despite the bartender calling after me, "C'mon, honey, have another!" I decided to leave the Spinning Wheel after that and not come back, well, ever. I'd recommend getting on this wheel only if you're very adventurous, or if you're a fiction writer seeking inspiration among these "real-life characters." (Note: Sac's, which serves the finest pizza I've had outside of Italy, is a block away.)

Perks: TVs, jukebox, fodder for your Bukowski-esque novel

Dive factor: 9

Stoned Crow

212-677-4022
85 Washington Place, at Sixth Avenue
Subway Directions: A/C/E/F/V/S to West 4th Street

The Stoned Crow is the kind of place that you could walk past for years without really noticing, and that's a shame because this West Village haunt is one of the friendliest bars in the city. Behind a small subterranean door there lies a long, dark bar and a back room with plenty of tables for eating, boozing and watching some serious pool playing. The unpretentious locals who inhabit the joint—a collection of aging frat boys, actors, firemen, layabouts, NYU students, and aspiring pool players who carry their own sticks—are more laid-back and cooler than the people you'll find at the tourist trap bars on nearby Bleecker Street.

Old concert posters and movie stills line the walls and the ceiling, and the bathrooms are the best-decorated dive bar bathrooms I've ever seen: rock photos in the men's room, and movie star pinups in the ladies' room. If you take a liking to vintage Paul Newman and Robert Redford, or shirtless Brad Pitt, or Speedo-clad Antonio Banderas, then bar-owner Betty, almost always lording over the pool table in the back, can provide you with copies to take home.

Of all the animal-named bars in the West Village—Blind Tiger, White Horse, Slaughtered Lamb, Kettle of Fish, Lion's Den—the Crow is the best.

Perks: TV, food, cigarettes, pool, creepy plastic crow behind the bar

Dive factor: 5

Subway Inn

Subway Inn

212-223-8929

143 E. 60th Street, at Lexington Avenue

Subway Directions: N/R/W to Lexington Avenue/59th Street., 4/5/6 to 59th Street

Don't be fooled: this bar is a stone's throw from Bloomingdale's, but you won't find the fashionista crowd in here. Case in point: the first time I came here, some gentlemen were trying to sell my pals and me stolen merchandise out of garbage bags. We politely declined.

This is more of a manly atmosphere—think retirees and veterans and assorted other hard-drinking men in a bar that's been around since the 1930s. Women are a rarer sighting. As is anyone who looks under 30. Maybe that's why even some of my heavy drinking associates never want to come here. Even dive bar regulars Sara and Nik vowed never to return with me to this nasty haunt, until they discovered that "Night Moves" (a song with a special place in their hearts—don't ask) was on the jukebox.

The same few old-timers are seemingly always here, along with an assortment of writers trying to soak up stories, cute loners, or a guy in gym shorts and a "wife-beater" tank top scarfing down a hero sandwich. Whatever you do, don't attempt to sit down at the booth with the very old owner; he won't appreciate your company.

The Subway Inn is not much to look at, but you're not looking for squeaky-clean environs, right? The A/C can be troublesome, and a busted window out front may not be fixed, and the red-and-black floor tiles are peeling and cracking, and the tables are wobbly. Look closely and you might even see bullet holes in the back from a shooting way back when.

Perks: jukebox

Dive factor: 8

Best for solo drinking

Blarney Cove
Red Rock West
Johnny's
Sophie's
International
Phoenix
Siberia

Sweetwater Tavern

718-963-0608
105 N. Sixth Street, between Berry Street and Wythe Street, Williamsburg, Brooklyn
Subway Directions: L to Bedford Avenue

Sometimes I hate going to Williamsburg—it can feel more like a *Nylon* magazine photo shoot than a place where real people live. But I'm happy to report that there are a few places left in this 'hood that aren't overrun by East Village emigrants drinking Mojitos and talking about their "art."

Sweetwater is a good bar in and of itself, made even better because it's a refuge from annoying Galapagos down the street. This punk rock haven is filled with an eclectic and pleasingly non-hip crowd (don't let the tattoos scare you, they're a friendly bunch). Depending on when you go, you will be mingling with either packs of punk boys (primarily on weekends), or regular Williamsburg residents (yes, they still exist!). The weeknight I was there I saw a couple having a conversation about racism, a regular moaning to the bartender about his rough day (standing in line to pay parking tickets—ouch!), and a Russian guy cursing to himself (in Russian).

If you don't want to listen to mult-lingual mutterings, the music is an incredible punk rock respite. Jukebox pics include staples like Lunachicks, Buzzcocks, Black Flag, Bad Brains, etc., plus a disc from the Heroin Sheiks, who I've admired for years just for their clever moniker. Any punk rocker worth his tongue piercing should make the trek here for the tunes alone.

The décor is a bit anomalous to the punk vibe—a quaint brownstone feel carried over by old-timey pictures on the walls, an old pressed tin ceiling, and dried corn (!) behind the cash register. The space is pleasingly dark, lit only by small wall sconces and a glaring spotlight above the cash register. As you head farther back, near the pool table and pinball and jukebox, things get divier, with plenty of graffiti. The ladies room was not a pretty picture: covered in graffiti, swelteringly hot, a mushy cigarette in the sink and a fly buzzing around.

Perks: pinball, pool, jukebox

Dive factor: 7

Three of Cups Lounge

212-388-2493
83 First Avenue, at 5th Street
Subway Directions: F/V to Second Avenue, 6 to Astor Place, L to First Avenue

This downstairs spot is perhaps a little too hip to be a real dive, but they have cans of Pabst ($2.50) in a bucket of ice on the bar, so that's good enough for me. This is a rock and roll hang out that never disappoints. I made my first trip here in 1996 and I'm happy to report that the same "Who the fuck is Mick Jagger?" poster is still on the wall, and the old mismatched couches haven't changed either. The place is hopping most nights, so you might have trouble scoring a couch or a seat at one of the tiny tables, but the vibe usually makes up for any crowd hassles. Off-times can be fun too—one Sunday night, two of my friends dropped ecstasy and then laid on the couches enjoying the typically impressive tunes.

There's not much room to dance in here, but my friend Michelle and I got our groove on one night to some T. Rex songs and nobody seemed to mind. Bartenders control the music (and do a damn fine job) unless there's a DJ. There's always a line for the bathrooms, but there's usually some cuties to chat with (of either sex) while you wait. And if you are feeling rebellious, the bathrooms at the Italian restaurant upstairs (also Three of Cups) are worth the climb.

The place is tiny without many frills—no TV, no pool table, no darts, or anything like that. Just a place to do some serious drinking and flirting (the candles and the red décor add to the sensual vibe). Shockingly, despite everybody in here partying like a rock star, I've never seen anybody stumble on the stairs leading to the lounge—don't be the first.

Perks: rocking music, food served in restaurant upstairs

Dive factor: 5

Turkey's Nest

718-384-9774
94 Bedford Avenue, at N. 10th Street, Williamsburg, Brooklyn
Subway Directions: L to Bedford Avenue

My friend Mike calls this bar "the U.N. of Trash," because so many variet-
ies (if not nationalities) of lowlife are welcomed here. And he's right—in
one evening, I found contractors, young sports fans, musicians, neighborhood regulars on a date, and some scary silk-shirted men at the pool table
all coexisting in peaceful inebriation. It seems that all walks of life can
appreciate a $2.50 pint of Bud (or $3.50 for a huge Styrofoam cup) and
the rotating $2 pint specials. Likewise, mixed drinks are served in manly-
sized plastic cups, not those wimpy little cocktail glasses you find at most
bars.

I always intend to stop in for just one drink at the Turkey's Nest, but the
friendly vibe and the generous buybacks usually keep me here for a few
hours. For you night owls, take note that the place can fill up a bit after 11.
And if you're an early riser with a strong stomach, you can start your day
here at 8 a.m. If you're bored with conversation at the bar, hit the pool
table, videogames, or Lotto machine. Friendly bartender Patrick can dish
up movie talk and tune the TVs to the rather un-divey Independent Film
Channel. The jukebox is standard, although I heard one too many Kenny
Rogers songs on a recent visit. My favorite thing about the bar, however, is
the "Turkettes" sign that decorates the door to the ladies room.

Perks: pool, lotto, pinball, bowling machine

Dive factor: 8

Most Old Men

Blarney Cove
Smith's
Danny O's
Holland
Subway Inn
Montero
Phil Hughes

Vazac's Horseshoe Bar (a.k.a. 7B)

212-473-8840
108 Avenue, at 7th Street
Subway Directions: L to First Avenue

Vazac's is not only a homey place for a few brews, it's also a great meeting point because any idiot can find it. Nobody really calls it Vazac's; everyone knows it as 7B, named for the prime corner that it's located on—Avenue B and Seventh St. , across the street from Tompkins Square Park.

No matter what time of day, or what day of the week, there always seems to be crowd well settled in at 7B. (Do new crowds keep coming in, or is it the same crowd, day after day after day?) Punks and sorority girls alike will find a comfortable home here. Plus the jukebox rocks and the lighting is festive.

The bar's horseshoe shape is kinda nifty (a pal of mine once said that the horseshoe made the place look like a bar from a movie, and in fact real filmmakers have used 7B—you may recognize it from films like *Serpico* and *Godfather II).* Loners and people on cheap dates usually settle at the front of the bar, while bigger groups of college kids settle into the tables and booths near the back and order plenty of pitchers. The large bar space coupled with the tiny two bathrooms means that there's quite often a line for the loo.

Not really the most earth-shaking place to visit, 7B is an easy-to-find spot to start your night, good for hooking up with friends who have a problem with directions. You will never have a particularly bad time here, nor a particularly good time. I find that my out-of-town guests always like 7B, as they find it (for some reason) emblematic of the quintessential East Village bar.

Perks: pinball, pitchers, jukebox, my friend Brian claims that he spotted Kelly Osbourne hanging here with a member of The Strokes

Dive factor: 4

Village Idiot

212-989-7334
355 W. 14th Street, between Eighth and Ninth Avenue
Subway Directions: A/C/E to 14th Street., L to 8th Avenue

My oh my, where do I start with this, the Disneyland of divebars? It's got blaringly loud country music, two-stepping old men mingling with frat boys, and it usually smells of vomit. It's also a Manhattan legend—the Village Idiot first opened in the '80s in the East Village, moving to this locale in the mid-90s.

The place fills up with aging frat boys and tourists who've heard the legend, plus a few hard-drinking locals who can stomach the obnoxiously loud country music (Hank Jr., Willie, Waylon). Bar dancing is permitted and encouraged, as is removing your necktie or bra. The place is downright obnoxious on Friday and Saturday nights, but if you roll in on, say, a Sunday afternoon, you'll have a much more relaxed time. The place often feels too contrived for its own good—you're more likely to see girls in twin sets and pearls "slumming it" than actual trailer trash—but it's a rowdy good time if you're in the mood. One-night stands are readily available, but I do know a pal who met a wealthy foreign businessman here and actually had an upstanding relationship with him for years. Still, their auspicious meeting had a hint of Idiot-style romance—his pickup line: "What can I get you?" My friend: "Cunnilingus." Asked and answered I guess!

Basically anything goes here—yellin', stompin', drinkin', fuckin'. One friend of mine once witnessed a drunk dude throwing a bottle at a female patron and *NOT* being asked to leave. There are a few nice, and real, touches, such as the old guy up front who tries to get pretty young things to do the two-step with him—go for it, he's a nice fellow.

Everyone should visit at least once—if only to run out screaming in horror. Before you sprint, chug a can of Pabst, do a shot with one of the buxom barmaids, or just grab a pitcher and retreat into your own tears-in-beer at one of the tables in the cavernous back room.

Perks: jukebox, pool, darts, pinball, free peanuts

Dive factor: 8

Village Idiot

Wakamba

212-244-9045
543 8th Avenue, between 37th and 38th Street
Subway Directions: A/C/E to 34th Street-Penn Station

The Wakamba can be a bit intimidating—or downright frightening. It's history is definitely sullied by the fact that in 2000, cops wrongly shot and killed a security guard, Patrick Dorismond, as he left the bar. The first time I tried to muster the courage to enter, I was already tipsy from an office party next door, but still didn't feel quite ready to sit down and have a beer here, as the place was filled with leering daylaborers mumbling to me in Spanish, and salsa music was pumping so loud I couldn't think. But to its credit, my most recent trip to the Wakamba was enjoyable. They have redone the décor (the awning out front now says "the distinguished Wakamba Lounge"), and now attract a classier clientele (not *too* classy, though—there were still a few guys eyeing the bartenders in hot pants).

Drinks are definitely overpriced, and at $5.25 for a bottle of Coors Light, you get to sit in a cheesy pleasure palace that Jack Lord would be proud of—we're talking fake grotto walls, mirrors, Hawaiian leis, plastic flowers, fake fish, and even a huge fake palm tree. No matter how hard they try, though, the Wakamba can't shake the seediness of the garment district. So drink up, watch your purse (figuratively and literally) and enjoy the feeling of Hawaii Dive-O. Book 'em, Danno!

Perks: jukebox, dance floor, fake palm trees, free peanuts at tables

Dive factor: 7

Cheapest Drinks

Blue & Gold
Mars Bar
Rudy's
Lys Mykyta
Bar 81 (Verk)
Holiday Cocktail Lounge

Walters

212-502-4023
389 Eighth Avenue, between 29th and 30th Street
Subway Directions: A/C/E to 34th Street-Penn Station

The friend that recommended Walters to me admitted that he used to hang out there early in the morning, after a full night of drinking. That's the kind of mindset I recommend before venturing into Walters—the place is best appreciated if you're already wasted.

Walters is definitely a bit rough around the edges—the dirty front door shouts "no soliciting/bathrooms for customers only." Still, it has more character than most of the other generic sports bars around Madison Square Garden, and Walters does appeal to some sports fans with its large TVs. If you'd rather play than watch, head for the dartboards or pool table in back. Restrooms, complete with doors falling off the hinges, are also back there.

The music is completely generic, Frampton coming alive as I arrived, "Stairway to Heaven" dying when I was departing. They even played the radio between tunes, complete with commercials. There's no draft, and mostly everyone chooses bottles of Bud as their drink of choice. My friend Chris and I opted for mixed drinks—$4.50 for a rather weak Absolut and tonic in one of those dumb wineglasses. Not a hipster in sight, the full bar had an old woman wearing a fanny pack, wearily rubbing her eyes, and men either speaking Spanish or sporting tattoos (or both).

Walters reminds me of some of the dives I've visited on Long Island. If you've never been to Long Island, just rent *Trees Lounge* to see what I'm talking about.

Perks: TVs, darts, pool, gumball machine, video games

Dive factor: 8

Serious Pool Tables

Alibi
Sophie's
Stoned Crow
Verk
Joe's
Night Cafe

Welcome to the Johnson's

212-420-9911
123 Rivington Street, between Essex Street and Norfolk Street
Subway Directions: F to Delancey Street, J/M/Z to Essex Street

I hesitated to include Welcome to the Johnson's because it's less of a dive and more of an *Ice Storm*-inspired theme bar (think suburban rec-room circa 1972, with wood paneling, plastic-covered furniture, and an old fridge). Still, any bar with trashy metal on the jukebox that serves $1.50 cans of a Pabst is a dive in *my* book.

Now that Johnson's has been open for a few years, some of the novelty has worn off, and many of the scene-seeking hipsters have ventured elsewhere in the Lower East Side, leaving in their wake a hearty group of neighborhood folks who know how to take advantage of a great happy hour that lasts until 9. The place is often packed, but on off-nights you'll find it uncrowded enough for entertainment. (I once played pool with a U.K. band in town to play on David Letterman, and, uh, played a bit more than pool with the drummer.) So put on your platform shoes, play "Smoke on the Water" on the jukebox, and throw your key chain into the hat. Mr. and Mrs. Johnson are feeling groovy!

Perks: jukebox, video games, pool

Dive factor: 3

Pabst Places

Bellevue
Three of Cups
Welcome to the Johnson's
Village Idiot
Doc Holliday's
Hank's
Yogi's

Yogi's

212-873-9852
2156 Broadway, at 76th Street
Subway Directions: 1/2/3 to 72nd Street

Leave it to my friend Kristyn (also known as Spesh) to introduce me to Yogi's, a little slice of redneck heaven in the otherwise genteel Upper West Side. Although she can be as classy as the next gal, Spesh also loves her country music, a little line dancing, and a few cans of Pabst. Yogi's (or Bear Bar as it is known by regulars who refuse to yield the old name to the other Bear Bar on the East Side) "bears" some resemblance to its down-town sister, the Village Idiot—buxom barkeeps, a few bras on the wall, a mostly country jukebox. The bar opens at 11:30 am, when you may find a few civil servants drowning their lunch hour sorrows, but things really pick up in the evening, when you'll find a mix of tourists, Ricki Lake show guests (from the Hotel Beacon), some regulars, and even a few soap stars from *One Life to Live*. Be warned, if there's a big show at the nearby Beacon Theater, the place may be too packed for your liking. Even if you can't stomach the crowds and all that Dolly Parton on the jukebox, you may want to brave it for the copious drink specials, or the $1.75 cans of Pabst and free peanuts.

Just be careful what all that Pabst might lead you to do—some regrettable bar dancing, or maybe taking home a New Zealand traveler who turned out by the harsh light of dawn to have "thrill me" tattooed on his chest. There are other hazards here as well, as my friend Pookie observed—she was here with a date when a fight broke out during the wee hours one morning. The instigator was thrown out, but not before leaving a trail of blood behind on the floor. The bouncer calmly wiped the blood off his leather jacket, and then Pook and her date assisted him in wiping the blood off a bar stool so another patron could sit down. (Maybe pack some anti-bacterial wipes and surgical gloves the next time you're headed here!)

Perks: Jukebox, bowls of peanuts, scantily clad female bartenders

Dive factor: 6

Yogi's

Triple Shots (Quick and Easy Dive Bar Crawls)

Milady's—162 Prince Street, at Thompson Street
Botanica—47 Houston Street, between Mott Street and Mulberry Street
Milano's—51 Houston Street, between Mott Street and Mulberry Street

Motor City—127 Ludlow Street, between Rivington and Delancey Street
169 Bar—169 East Broadway, between Rutgers Street and Jefferson Street
Parkside Lounge—317 East Houston Street, between Avenues B and C

Hogs & Heifers— 859 Washington Street, at 13th Street
Village Idiot—355 West 14th Street, between Eighth and Ninth Avenue
Red Rock West—457 West 17th Street, at Tenth Avenue

Jimmy's Corner—140 W. 44th Street, between Broadway and 6th Ave.
Smith's—701 Eighth Avenue, at 44th Street
Siberia—356 West 40th Street, at Ninth Avenue

Phoenix—447 East 13th Street, between First Avenue and Avenue A
The Bar—68 Second Avenue, at 4th Street
The Cock—188 Avenue A, at 12th Street

Barrows Pub—463 Hudson Street, at Barrow Street
Johnny's—90 Greenwich Avenue, between 12th and 13th Street
Village Idiot—355 West 14th Street, between Eight and Ninth Avenue

Holland Bar—532 Ninth Avenue, between 39th and 40th Street
Bellevue—538 Ninth Avenue, at 40th Street
Rudy's—627 Ninth Avenue, between 44th and 45th Street

O'Connor's—39 Fifth Avenue, between Bergen and Dean Street, Bklyn
Freddy's—485 Dean Street, at 6th Avenue, Bklyn
Alibi—242 DeKalb Avenue, at Vanderbilt Avenue, Bklyn

Blue & Gold—79 East 7th Street, between 1st and 2nd Avenue
Bar 81 (Verk)—81 East 7th Street, at First Avenue
International—120 1/2 First Avenue, between 6th and 7th Street

Raccoon Lodge—1439 York Avenue, between 76th and 77th Street
American Trash—1471 First Avenue, between 76th and 77th Street
Reif's—302 E. 92nd Street, between First and Second Avenue

Mona's—224 Avenue B, between 13th and 14th Street
O'Hanlon's-349 E. 14th Street, between First and Second Avenue
Blarney Cove—510 East 14th Street, between Avenues A and B

O'Hanlon's-349 E. 14th Street, between First and Second Avenue
(Then one L-train stop to Bedford Avenue)
Sweetwater—105 N. Sixth Street, between Berry and Wythe Street, Bklyn
Turkey's Nest—94 Bedford Avenue, and North 10th Street, Bklyn

[Starting easy, ending divey, West]
Ear Inn—326 Spring Street, between Hudson Street and Greenwich Street
Nancy Whiskey—1 Lispenard Street, at West Broadway
Baby Doll Lounge—34 White Street, at Church Street

[Starting easy, ending divey, East]
Grassroots Tavern—20 St. Mark's Place, between 2nd and 3rd Avenue
Lucy's—135 Avenue A, between St. Mark's Street and 9th Street
Mars Bar—25 East 1st Street, at Second Avenue

INDEX
By Location and Page Number

Houston Street to 14th Street, East

Houston Street to 14th Street, West

14th Street to 50th street

Above 50th Street

QUEENS

STATEN ISLAND

Grassroots Tavern